MW00346037

NO LONGER PROPERTY OF
ANYTHINK LIBRARIES/
RANGEVIEW LIBRARY DISTRICT

Paranormal Research:
A Comprehensive Guide to
Building a Strong Team

by Jack Kenna

4880 Lower Valley Road • Atglen, PA 19310

The author's parents John Joseph Kenna Jr. and Helen Catherine Kenna (Milos) circa early 1950s in front of Helen's family home in Troy, New York.

This book is dedicated to my father, John Joseph Kenna Jr., and my mother, Helen Catherine Kenna (Milos). Thanks Ma for sharing your own spiritual and paranormal experiences with me, for listening to my own, and for sharing your insights on them. Thanks to you and Dad for always teaching us kids to keep an open mind, trust in our faith, and to always do what we believed was right, even if it was the more difficult path to follow.

Copyright © 2018 by Jack Kenna

Library of Congress Control Number: 2017955196

All rights reserved. No part of this work may be reproduced or used in any form or by any means—graphic, electronic, or mechanical, including photocopying or information storage and retrieval systems—without written permission from the publisher.

The scanning, uploading, and distribution of this book or any part thereof via the Internet or any other means without the permission of the publisher is illegal and punishable by law. Please purchase only authorized editions and do not participate in or encourage the electronic piracy of copyrighted materials.

"Schiffer," "Schiffer Publishing, Ltd.," and the pen and inkwell logo are registered trademarks of Schiffer Publishing, Ltd.

Cover design by Brenda McCullum
Type set in Helvetica Neue & Minion Pro.

* Unless otherwise noted, all photos and images are the property of the author.

ISBN: 978-0-7643-5526-4
Printed in China

Published by Schiffer Publishing, Ltd.
4880 Lower Valley Road
Atglen, PA 19310
Phone: (610) 593-1777; Fax: (610) 593-2002
E-mail: Info@schifferbooks.com
Web: www.schifferbooks.com

For our complete selection of fine books on this and related subjects, please visit our website at www.schifferbooks.com. You may also write for a free catalog.

Schiffer Publishing's titles are available at special discounts for bulk purchases for sales promotions or premiums. Special editions, including personalized covers, corporate imprints, and excerpts, can be created in large quantities for special needs. For more information, contact the publisher.

We are always looking for people to write books on new and related subjects. If you have an idea for a book, please contact us at proposals@schifferbooks.com.

Contents

Acknowledgments...4

Introduction 5

Chapter 1 – Investigating the Paranormal 7

Chapter 2 – Communicating with Spirits..................................11

Chapter 3 – Working with Clients 17

Chapter 4 – Collecting Client Information 23

Chapter 5 – Conducting an Investigation................................28

Chapter 6 – Reviewing Evidence and Reporting Findings 35

Chapter 7 – Equipment 45

    The Digital Audio Recorder...46

    Digital Audio Editing Software.......................................53

    The Mel Meter 55

    Closed-Circuit Television Digital Video Recorders 57

    DVR Systems and the Paranormal 58

    EPODS..65

    Photography..68

    The Advent of Spirit Photography 69

    The Pros and Cons of Digital Camera Technology................69

    Digital Camera Choices...71

    Laser Grids 73

    Electromagnetic Pump 76

    The Ovilus® 80

    Ghost Radar® Application...85

    Thermal Imaging Cameras 88

    Protecting and Organizing Your Equipment 92

    The Human Factor...94

Investigations of S.P.I.R.I.T.S. of New England 102

Chapter 8 – The Deane Winthrop House.................................104

Chapter 9 – The Houghton Mansion 112

Chapter 10 – The Fairbanks House.......................................129

Chapter 11 – The USS *Constitution* (Old Iron Sides) 149

Final Thoughts..181

Bibliography 182

Worksheets...183

Acknowledgments

I would first like to thank Schiffer Publishing, especially Peter Schiffer and Dinah Roseberry, for providing me with the opportunity, tools, and encouragement to publish my work; this dream of mine would not have come to life without you and the rest of the staff at Schiffer Publishing. Thanks also to my friends Katie Boyd and Beckah Boyd, who not only encouraged me to write, but have also helped me on my personal journey into the world of the paranormal, helping me to open my mind and spirit to the knowledge that we all have our own unique abilities and that once we embrace them anything is possible. My deepest thanks and love to my extended family, S.P.I.R.I.T.S. of New England®—Ellen, Beck, Sharon, and Sarah—thank you for giving me the opportunity to be a part of this great team and family; thank you for your faith in me, and for your forgiveness when it is needed; thank you for all the good and bad times we have shared over the years and the ones we will share in the years to come; and thank you for allowing me to be the "jerk" I know I sometimes can be, but loving me in spite of it. A special thank you to my friend, Dustin Pari; you are a good man, a good friend, and an inspiration to many. Thank you to the US Navy and the 2010 commander, officers, and crew of the USS Constitution ("Old Ironsides") in Charlestown, Massachusetts, for allowing us to investigate this great and proud ship for them in July 2010; it was and still is a true honor to have assisted you, and to have had the unique honor to have been the first ever paranormal team to investigate this historic ship. Special thanks to Boatswain Mate 2nd Class (BM2) Philip Gagnon and Aviation Boatswain's Mate Aircraft Handler Airman (ABHN) Mark Alexander for both spending a night as our escort on the ship while knowing they still had to fulfill additional duties the next day, as well as missing out on time from family and friends. Their professionalism and knowledge of the ship and its history made the success of our investigation possible, and reflects great credit upon themselves, their ship, their crew, their commander, and the US Navy. Thank you to the Fairbanks House Historical Site, the Fairbanks Family in America, and the board of directors for allowing us the opportunity to investigate their wonderful and historic Fairbanks Family House in Dedham, Massachusetts, and for allowing us this true honor to share some of the history of the home and family, photos, and the findings of our investigation in this book. Lastly, a very special thank you to my family and friends who encouraged me in this endeavor; I could not have done this without your encouragement and inspiration.

Introduction

The abbreviation S.P.I.R.I.T.S. in our team name S.P.I.R.I.T.S. of New England® stands for Super-natural, Paranormal, Investigations, Research, Intuitive, Truth, Society. I will just stick with referring to us as S.P.I.R.I.T.S. for most of the remainder of this book so it is easier on all of us, but at least now you know what it stands for.

S.P.I.R.I.T.S. of New England was founded on the tenth of January in the year 2009 by Ms. Ellen MacNeil and co-founders Beck Gann and Sharon Koogler. The original team consisted of eight team members: Ellen, Beck, Sharon, Ellen's daughter Sarah Campbell, and four of their friends. All of them met through an online paranormal forum, the same one that I would later meet them all on as well. Two of the friends lived in a southern state and two others lived in the Boston area. I first met them all through the online forum around the end of 2008, just before they officially founded their team. As with all paranormal teams there came growing pains and personality issues, and eventually the original team dwindled down to just four: Ellen, Beck, Sarah, and Sharon. Before that happened, I met my friends for the first time at a ghost hunting event in New Hampshire at the Spalding Inn. It was at this event that Ellen MacNeil left me with a unique and lasting first impression. I was standing on the front porch of the Inn when a car pulled up. I had seen photos of Ellen on the forum, so I knew what she looked like, but I have to admit that nothing could have prepared me for what I was about to see climb out of the back seat of that car. There, with bird feathers in her hair and on her S.P.I.R.I.T.S. black hoodie, speckled with blood and wearing a pouty face as she looked up at me, was Ellen MacNeil. Without a word she climbed up the stairs toward me, still pouting, still covered in the remains of a poor little bird. Behind her, her daughter Sarah yelled up that they had just hit a bird that came through the partially opened back window where Ellen was sitting, and it literally exploded all over her! I could not help but begin to smile and laugh. I looked at Ellen, opened my arms wide, and gave my new friend a big hug, bird, feathers, blood, and all! She has been like a sister to me ever since.

That weekend was just the beginning of what would turn into a life-changing journey for our small team. Although we all had a great time, it would be many more months before I would finally be made a member of the team, and during that time there would be some serious clashes between some of the original members of the team to the point where S.P.I.R.I.T.S. itself would almost fade into oblivion as so many other teams had that sprouted up during the paranormal revival of the early twenty-first century. The team weathered their storm and came out on the other side a solid, close-knit family of five seasoned investigators that have earned the respect of their peers in the paranormal community. I am very proud and honored to be a member of this team, and would not be writing this book today if it had not been for the acceptance, support, and encouragement of my S.P.I.R.I.T.S. family. Thank you so much Ellen, Beck, Sharon, and Sarah for allowing me not only on to your team, but into your lives.

CHAPTER 1
Investigating the Paranormal

Since the human race first developed the ability of higher cognitive process, we have strived to understand things that are above our current level of comprehension. When we first gazed up at the billions of stars in our sky they were far beyond our understanding of our world; we had no concept of space, star systems, galaxies, or the universe. Early humanity was frightened of the night sky, but there were a few who strove to better understand it, to observe it, and as ages passed, those few humans who investigated this literally untouchable and enormous mystery were able to find consistency in it, make some sense of it, and make use of it—even if only on what we today would consider a small scale—but it was very useful to those early humans for determining the best times of the year to plant and later harvest their crops. Had it not been for these few inquisitive early humans that looked up at the stars not in fear, but in wonder and curiosity, we would not have the science we know today as astronomy. This can be said for all of the accumulated knowledge through mathematics, the sciences, and technologies that we now reap the benefits of.

While many of the main stream sciences of today can trace their roots back to individual early humans that dedicated their lives to researching what in their time was considered by most people in their cultures to be foolishness or even dangerous, these same main stream sciences now look upon research in the field of the paranormal the same way. They consider it foolish, a waste of time and resources, and in some cases they have seen it as a threat to their long established theories and self-imposed facts. Some insist the existence of ghosts—or the human soul if you will—and life after death can never be proven. Perhaps they are right, perhaps they are not. Those of us who seriously pursue this field of research would respond to these remarks with the same optimism and open-mindedness of those same early founders of the sciences, and we say to our skeptics, "That has yet to be substantiated."

If there is one thing that the twenty-first century field of paranormal research has been able to substantiate, it is the number of self-proclaimed paranormal investigators and teams that suddenly popped up overnight during the first season of a popular reality television show that aired in the early part of the twenty-first century. I am not saying that this show was in any way a detriment to paranormal research; just the opposite in fact, as it was the first television show that ever dealt seriously with what true paranormal research is like, what it attempts to do, and how it is actually carried out—at least as best as it could within a one-hour time slot. The only minor issue is that this show and other similar shows that came after it may have given birth to people who had no prior interest nor experience in the paranormal, but instead looking at it as a way to quickly gain fame and fortune by trying to get on the show, or trying to get a show of their own. These self-proclaimed paranormal experts were creating teams in an attempt to get rich quick. This is not to say that there were no groups that blossomed out of this paranormal revival that did not have a true passion for the field, and for trying to conduct relevant investigations, collect serious data, attempt to find real answers, and help people in the process, all at no cost to the people they assist and with no ego involved. S.P.I.R.I.T.S. of New England is one of these teams. I would also be remiss if I did not acknowledge the many paranormal teams and groups that were already in existence doing great work in this field long before the reality TV shows came along.

As for S.P.I.R.I.T.S., we conduct investigations and research not just for the sake of research, but to try and find answers for our clients, and to help them not only understand their experiences, but also understand that not everything they may be experiencing is paranormal and not all ghosts/spirits are demons as depicted on television and in movies.

Investigating the paranormal is not something to be taken lightly, to do in hopes of getting a television show and becoming famous, or in the hopes of getting an adrenaline rush out of being scared by something in the dark. If any of these are the reason you want to investigate the paranormal, then do not bother creating or joining a team, because you are doing it for the wrong reasons. You are also just going to waste your time and money on something you will do once or twice, then get bored or disillusioned as you find out what is really involved in paranormal investigating. I am not saying these things to be harsh, but for those of you who have bought a digital recorder, video camera, or some type of Electro-Magnetic Field (EMF) meter, answer these three questions for yourself: How long ago did you buy these items? How many investigations have you gone on? How much of the audio and video you collected during an investigation have you taken time to review to see if you caught any evidence, such as Electronic Voice Phenomena (EVPs)?

To me, the most important of those three questions is the last one. Even if you have only been on one investigation, if you never bothered to listen to or watch the several hours of audio and video you took on that investigation then why did you even bother investigating? The truth is ninety percent or more of paranormal evidence is only found during review of data—audio, video, and photos—collected during an investigation. Sitting in the dark in an old abandoned building waiting to be frightened by odd noises like bangs, thumps, scratching, knocks, etc., is not paranormal investigation. It is also trespassing if you did not gain permission from the owner to be there. None of these things are of any benefit to serious paranormal research; in fact, they are a detriment to our field of research. It is what gives paranormal researchers a bad name and makes it very difficult to legally gain access to locations to conduct serious research. If you are one of those rare individuals that after spending an evening investigating a supposed haunted location—legally or not—spent at least a couple hours reviewing your audio, video, and photos for possible evidence of the paranormal, and you found that you did not mind taking the time to do it just on the chance that you may find an EVP or something strange on your video or in a photo, then I would say you just might have a real interest in investigating the paranormal. My suggestion to you would be to take the next step and at least go to a paranormal event. It does not have to be an investigation; many serious teams hold fundraising events for historical locations they investigate. These fundraisers are a great way to meet and talk with serious paranormal investigators about your own experiences and even spend a night investigating with them during an event. Most paranormal events do offer an evening investigation as part of the fundraiser. You can also contact paranormal teams through their websites or Facebook® pages to ask them questions, or see if they are looking for new team members, or holding any type of public events or lectures that will allow you to investigate with them. Our own team tries to offer a free lecture and investigation once or twice a year which is open to the public. The number of people allowed to the investigation is limited to twenty, but it does offer people the opportunity to experience a real investigation at no cost, as well as see and hear real paranormal evidence that our team has gathered on various investigations. We teach the people who are with us how to investigate: we show them how to investigate, give them pointers, show them how to check out sounds and noises to determine if they are something natural or if it might be paranormal, and then we let them conduct the investigation with one of our team members there to observe, answer questions, and assist them if they like. It is a learning experience. We are not the only team to hold these types of events, as many serious teams all over the country do.

CHAPTER 2
Communicating with Spirits

As a technical specialist and case manager for my team, I field many different questions from various clients and people interested in ghost hunting. Their questions are numerous and varied, everything from the typical "Do ghosts really exist?" to "How do I get rid of the demon in my house?" The most common question I am asked is, "How do I communicate with the ghost in my house?" I find this to be one of the most interesting, complicated, and provocative questions I am asked. You might ask me why I think this. First, it is an interesting question, because the person asking is already assuming, or is convinced that they have a ghost in their home; or, as a potential or new investigator, they have predisposed themselves to believing a spirit is present before they have even investigated. Second, it is complicated because I am about to respond to someone who typically knows nothing or very little about the paranormal or this field of study, but they are already convinced they are dealing with a ghost. Third, it is provocative because of all the questions I receive, this one can even set seasoned paranormal investigators at odds with each other on how to communicate with those who have passed on, or even if direct communication should be attempted at all. Given these considerations, the following are my own thoughts and approach on how to communicate with people both living and dead.

What I just wrote is exactly how I personally approach the topic of attempting to communicate with those who have died but still linger among us. As a famous investigator once told me when I was starting out in this field, "Ghosts were people too." This statement, with the exception of demons, nature spirits, or other non-human spirits, is very accurate for the majority of spirits we may encounter as paranormal investigators. These human spirits were people like you and me that are now deceased. They once had families, jobs, emotions, problems, issues, and baggage just like the rest of us. So why not deal with them and talk to them just like we do living people? For me, this is exactly what I always try to do and what I suggest to others. There is much more to it than just talking, though. I also believe that body language and tone of voice play a big part in talking with the dead, just as much as it does with the living. Remember, from what we know so far as investigators, even though we cannot see spirits, they often seem to be able to see us. The following is my approach and guidelines for attempting communication with potential spirits, and people for that matter.

1. Do not assume there is a spirit in the location you are investigating. This may seem odd or even crazy to some of you, (i.e., then what the heck am I about to try to communicate with?). The point here is do not get your expectations up that you are going to get a response or have a two-way conversation; it just does not happen that way, and you are going to get bored very quickly and give up way too soon if you have high expectations to talk with a ghost.

2. Relax. Sit down, lean against a wall, and just get comfortable, as if you are about to have a conversation with a friend.

3. Take a nonconfrontational posture. Do not cross your arms tightly or sit hunched over in a ball; these are postures that indicate you are not open to conversation or any type of interaction, and could even be considered defensive. If you are standing, keep your arms loosely at your sides with your hands slightly outward, or if you cross your arms, keep them loosely crossed with your hands showing outside on your elbows. If you are sitting down, lean back with your hands on top of your legs with your palms up. Both of these postures indicate you are nondefensive, nonconfrontational, and open to listening and talking. If you are sitting, it is OK to lean forward with your arms still out on top of your legs and your palms up. This position actually indicates you are very interested in hearing what the other person has to say. The most important thing here is to appear as physically nonthreatening and as open to conversation as possible. People are generally more likely to engage in conversation with someone they do not know who appears to be friendly, open, and outgoing than someone who seems to be crabby, angry, upset, or just plain snobbish.

4. When speaking, be friendly, calm, quiet, and even happy in your tone of voice. Do not start by being demanding or asking demanding questions, such as, "Tell me your name." Try a more friendly approach; just as with a live person, introduce yourself first, "Hello my name is . . . can you please tell me your name?" Some investigators believe that it is dangerous to give out your name to spirits, as they believe it can empower the spirit to have an advantage over you. This may or may not be true, but I personally look at it from the perspective that as spirits, if there is one there, they already have a big advantage over me in many ways, so I do not see how trying to be polite and giving them my first name can give them that much more of an advantage. I personally have never had a problem with at least giving out my first name, although just to be on the safe side I never use my last name. During an investigation good team members are always tagging who is in and/or investigating a room by identifying each member by their first name, so your name has already been tossed in. Again, the point here is to start off by being polite and friendly. Most people when you introduce yourself will also introduce themselves to you. As you carry on your conversation and questioning be considerate of and think about what this bodiless person may be feeling and thinking. Yes, I said "feeling and thinking." If you are dealing with a possible intelligent haunting then you must accept the fact that a spirit is capable of emotions and thought. I believe that in these types of hauntings, the spirit or spirits involved still maintain the personalities, feelings, and perhaps even mental state of mind they had when they were alive. I believe this is at least a good assumption to go by when attempting to communicate; like a person you never met before, you just do not know what type of personality or individual you are dealing with until you have spent some time with them. In dealing with a potential spirit, it is even more of a question, as you may not know if you are even talking with someone until after the investigation is done and you review the audio, photo, and video data you have collected.

5. Be very patient. Patience in this field of work is a *big* virtue. Even for an experienced investigator, it can literally take hours before getting any type of response that might indicate the presence of

any type of paranormal activity, let alone the presence of a true intelligent spirit. Most of the time nothing is experienced during an investigation, or only one or two of the team members will experience something out of the ordinary.

6. Be vigilant. Pay close attention to your surroundings, what is there, and any changes. This can make the difference between knowing if something is trying to communicate with you or not. This is also very true for paying attention to what your body and senses are telling you. Many paranormal investigators, including myself, believe that *you* are the best piece of investigative equipment you have. Your body is very sensitive to even small changes in temperature, humidity, air density, gravity, and even electromagnetic fluctuations and fields. Use your senses. When you enter a room, sit down, relax, and *feel* the room. Is it cold, hot, warm, humid, dry? Is the air heavy, light, dense, etc.? What sounds are in the room, what light is entering the room? Changes in any of these things could be an indication that something out of the ordinary is happening. But what does this have to do with communication? Since it is much more difficult to talk with someone that you can't see or hear than it is someone sitting right in front of you, you must rely on what you can see, hear, and feel to help you carry on a hopefully interesting and engaging conversation. For instance, since it is likely that any possible spirit you are trying to communicate with lived in, or at least is somehow attached to, the building or grounds you are investigating, look around to see what is there. Is there something about the building or area that you can bring up in conversation that they might be interested in or that might be important to them? This is why it is also good to know at least some of the history of the building or area you are investigating so you can use it in your attempt to communicate. Since it is rare to actually hear a verbal response, listen for noises that seem out of place, or try to sense changes in the area you are investigating that might indicate someone is trying to communicate with you, or that you hit on a subject matter that perhaps has caught the interest of whomever might be there.

7. Ask relevant, concise, lucid, and friendly questions. When you are talking with a friend or stranger, your conversation always follows a specific train of thought regarding a topic you are discussing. If you ask a question, it is always relevant to the subject being discussed, and your questions are typically short and to the point as you attempt to get an answer. When attempting to contact a spirit, you are typically asking questions to try and obtain a response. In this case, it is very important to maintain a line of questioning, keep to a subject matter, and keep the questions short and clear. The following is an example of a line of questioning I like to use when attempting to talk with a potential spirit.

a. Hello, my name is Jack.
b. I was invited by the other people who live here to come and try to talk with you. Could you please come close and talk with me?
c. Can you please tell me your name?
d. I work for ____. Can you tell me what work you do or did?
e. I love my job. Do or did you like yours?
f. My job does not make me rich, but it helps me support my family. Do you have a family?

This should at least give you an idea of what I am getting at. In the last question, you can also see how I use this simple line of questioning to expand the conversation and lead into the new topic of family from the topic of work. The transition is fairly smooth; even though I am really having a one-sided conversation, the train of thought still flows evenly and would be very similar to a conversation I might have with a person that I just met for the first time. What you do not want to do is jump from one topic to another in a mess of jumbled questions. The following is an example of a poor line of questioning.

a. What is your name?
b. Why are you here?
c. When did you die?
d. How did you die?
e. Why do you stay here?
f. Why do you haunt this place?

Although these questions may seem clear and concise, they are rude and jumbled. Think of it this way: if someone you never met before just sat down in your home and started asking you questions like this, how would you react? Personally, I would be pretty darn offended and would tell them to leave or get out! Maybe that is why we investigators get that EVP so often. I am sure you have noticed that I have focused on positive communication, but many of you may be asking, "What about provoking to get a response?" I do believe that provoking does have a place when investigating, but in my opinion provoking does not mean being abusive. Provoking can be as simple as saying something like, "Well, I think it is pretty rude that I came all this way to talk with you and you will not respond to me!" or "If you are not going to talk with me then I am leaving, I am not going to waste any more of my time on you." I do not believe in swearing or being verbally abusive. Although I do know that some investigators believe this technique works best, I disagree. Like with living people, when you become verbally abusive to someone they tend to become negative themselves, and then shut down, so to speak. You may get one quick immediate knee-jerk reaction, but then they take off and do not speak to you again. If part of our purpose here as paranormal investigators is to try and communicate with those who have passed on then we should want to try and keep the communication going for as long as possible to try and gather as much data to validate the existence of the paranormal. Provoking does not help accomplish this, and in the case where a client is involved, abusive verbal provocation can possibly cause even more problems for the client if they are experiencing a true haunting, because now that spirit may be very upset and could take its anger and frustration out on the client since the investigator is no longer there. Just as any typical living person does when they are angry or upset, we tend to take our frustrations out on others. Again, I encourage you to remember that ghosts were people, too. Try talking to them with the same level of respect and compassion that you would any living person. By doing so, you just might find that you not only get potential responses from any spirits that might be present, but you may also find that you have more fun, that feel better about your investigations, and that your clients are impressed by the professionalism of you and your team.

CHAPTER 3
Working with Clients

At some point most paranormal teams advance themselves from investigating public places to conducting client investigations. Most of the time this transition is done by the team with very little to no training or experience on how to work with private clients. It is this lack of knowledge dealing with clients that often ends up breaking a team, or at least causing major headaches and problems, even sometimes legal ones. They also often end up with a bad reputation of being unorganized and unprofessional. My focus in these next few chapters will be to give some insight into what is involved with working with private clients and what you need to know and do to successfully work with them while building a strong team with a good reputation.

Although not necessarily the first thing you should know or learn when you decide to transition your team from public investigations to client investigations, I believe the human factor is the most important to consider. What am I referring to? What do I mean by the human factor? The human factor takes into account the personalities, mental condition, physical condition, and communication skills of the client(s), as well as the members of your team and their abilities/capabilities to successfully interact with each other and your clients. These are the things we deal with every day when dealing with family, coworkers, and strangers. Who we are and our ability to successfully communicate and interact with each other have a direct impact on the outcome of any situation we may find ourselves in.

Clients, like paranormal investigators, come in all shapes, sizes, cultural backgrounds, ethnicities, educational levels, and financial status. They turn to paranormal teams for a unique type of help that they just can't find any place else. The type of problems these clients believe they have can't be solved by a plumber, electrician, engineer, psychologist, doctor, or handyman, and yet it can take all of these talents to truly solve the problems that these clients are dealing with. As a paranormal investigator, it is extremely important to remember that even though your client may not be paying you for the help you provide, they have high expectations of you to help them solve their problem. Once you agree to take their case, you have a professional obligation to do the best job you can for them, and for your team to give one hundred percent effort, even to the point of admitting to the client that their case may be beyond your team's abilities and to refer them to a team or other type of professional that can help them. Being honest and open with your clients is very important to helping your client and building a good reputation for your team.

Although it is important for you to be honest and open with your clients, your clients will not always be honest and open with you. People have motives for everything they do. Your motives for being a paranormal investigator and working with clients may be anything from just wanting to gain more knowledge and experience with the paranormal to enjoying helping people. A client's motives for requesting that you investigate their home may range from just wanting to meet a ghost hunter to something a bit more selfish and dark, such as trying to obtain some type of financial gain and attention. Some clients even think they can capture a bit of fame if you say their house is haunted, because they think they can end up on television. The point to remember here is that not every client's motives are pure. This is why it is very important to gather as much pre-investigation information from a client as possible to try and verify their reasons for requesting your help, and to try and provide the best assistance you can. After gathering this information, you may even decide that you do not want to take the client's case, or the potential client may not even fill out or return the requested information form at all. On the team I belong to, we make it very clear to any potential client that if you do not fill out our information form then we can't help you. I cannot tell you how many times I never hear back from a potential client after sending them our form, which tells me that they most likely do not need our help. (I will cover more about the form I am talking about in the next chapter, but let us just say for now that the client information form is about ten pages long and asks for such personal information as current medications, physical and mental health, possible drug abuse, etc.)

Let us say the client has answered all of your questions and seems to be honest with their answers, and you decide to take their case. What should you do next? Call the client and go over the information they provided with them. You are sure to have a few questions for them, and they will definitely have questions for you. Making the phone call will also give all parties the opportunity to get a better feeling for the type of persons and personalities you are dealing with. Is this person easygoing? Under a lot of stress? Are they truly scared or upset by what they are experiencing, and do they seem sincere? These are things you will only be able to get a feel for by talking with them. This is true when dealing with anyone, but it is especially important when working with a client. It is very important to build a professional and friendly rapport with them to make them feel at ease with allowing you into their home or business, and to establish a sense of trust with them. You want your clients to trust you, so that when you finish your investigation and provide them with your findings they will at least take your findings seriously, and accept any recommendations you may make even if what you reveal to them is not what they expected or wanted to hear. This brings up another important thing to remember when working with a client. For the most part, by the time a client has finally contacted your team they have typically already made up their mind that their home is haunted, and may even provide you with the names and descriptions of the spirits that are there. Now you come in and conduct an investigation, and perhaps find no evidence of paranormal activity at all. What you discover is that their experiences are being caused by their medications, pipes banging, chemical fumes, high EMF, etc. Your client's reaction to these findings could possibly be very negative unless you have gained their confidence in advance. If you have, they may not totally agree with your findings, but they will at least listen to you and accept some of what you have found, especially those things that may be a hazard within their property, such as high levels of EMF or carbon monoxide.

Gaining the trust and confidence of your client is key to working with them successfully, but be careful how you do this. Everyone has their own motivations for doing things, and most clients have already made up their minds that their home or business is haunted. What they are really looking for you to do is validate what they believe is going on. When you make that first phone call to a client or respond to that first e-mail from them, be very careful not to agree with or validate what they are telling you is happening in their home. If a client tells you that they had a coffee cup fly off their kitchen table, see shadow people walking in their hallways, have been touched by something they can't see, or are hearing voices talking upstairs when no one else is home and they know it has to be a ghost, *do not* say to them, "Yes, it sure seems like you might have something paranormal going on." If you do, you may have just gained their trust in you, but you have also just backed yourself into a corner, because what they just heard you say was, "Yes, your home is haunted." You have just validated their belief, and if you investigate and find nothing, they are going to be confused and upset—to them you and your team do not know what you are doing. A good approach when working with a client that is convinced their property is haunted is to listen to them, and let them tell you what they think is going on. Then ask them why they think they have a spirit in their home and ask them for specifics of an experience they had. You will find them pushing you a bit to tell them they have a ghost or are experiencing paranormal activity, but do not. Clients will typically tell me an experience they had, such as they had their coffee cup move across their kitchen table, and then say to me, "I know that is what spirits can do, right?" I will respond to this question/statement by discussing with the client some of the theories that exist in the paranormal community as to possible normal and paranormal causes of this type of activity. I also usually take this opportunity to tell the client that although I understand they may believe they are experiencing something paranormal, I know nothing about their home, have not been there, and most importantly, have not investigated it yet, so I cannot tell them if they are experiencing anything paranormal or not. I will then tell them that it is also possible that there are more normal causes for what they are experiencing. At this point I usually get a disappointed sounding "Oh" from the client, followed by some resistance to my statement, more discussion about their experiences, and questions about other investigations our team has done and what we found. By taking this approach with the client you accomplish several things.

1. You have let them know that your team does not make any decisions until after you have investigated and reviewed the data collected. This establishes your team's credibility with the client that you will do a thorough investigation and provide them with actual findings.

2. It has opened the door for active discussions with the client about your team's experience, as well as allowing you to provide the client with some educational information on real paranormal theories and natural causes for what they believe are paranormal experiences. Remember, what almost all clients know about the paranormal is from what they have seen on television or in the movies.

3. By opening this dialogue, you have begun to gain their trust by letting them know that your team will be honest with them, and will do all that you can to help them identify the actual causes of their experiences and help resolve them.

Now that you have established a good relationship with your client, it is important to maintain that relationship. To do this, I strongly recommend maintaining one formal point of contact on the team for the client. This should be the team member who made the first phone contact with the client, your case manager. This will foster a stronger bond between your team and the client, as it will make the client feel more at ease/comfortable dealing with the same person, at least up until the first face-to-face meeting between your team and the client. So how do you decide which member of your team is best suited to have first contact with any potential clients? Who should be the team's case manager? This falls to individual team member personalities—the human factor. Since the person you choose to be your case manager will be dealing directly with clients, and will be the key person that represents your team to your clients, you want to choose someone who has people skills, someone who is friendly, outgoing, confident, and has a good working knowledge of your team, its members, the paranormal, and debunking. The last four skills can be learned, but it is important that the team member you choose possesses the first four personality traits to ensure the best chance of successful first contact and continued positive interaction with your clients. In essence, your case manager is your public relations officer between your team and your clients. They can make or break your team.

Regardless of how good or great a case manager you have, there is always the chance that you can run into a client that could have some serious mental health issues, so you need to be very careful what contact information you provide to a client. Never post personal addresses or phone numbers of your team members on your website, and never provide them to a client no matter how comfortable or friendly you may feel with them. Use a post office box for any mail communication, or even better, use an e-mail address that is specifically set up for your team with your team's name. For phone contact, provide a cell phone number or an 800 number for your clients. *Never* invite a client to your home or workplace, because if you do run into a client that has some serious issues you can put yourself and your family in real danger. Always meet the client at their home and never go alone; always have at least one other team member with you when you go to meet with a client. If something does not seem right when you meet with them and you feel that you should not take the case, then politely excuse yourself, leave the client's home, and do not go back. If you feel you need to, you can send them a follow-up e-mail stating that you are unable to take their case for personal reasons or due to other obligations.

The things I have discussed so far are just some of the human factors you need to consider before deciding to work with clients. Working and dealing with clients in the paranormal field is a fascinating, complicated, sometimes dangerous, and almost always rewarding endeavor, but it is not for everyone, nor even every team. Before making this decision for your team, sit down with all of your members and discuss it. The personalities of your team members will come into play. Some will be all for it, others may be reluctant or want more information before they make their decision, and still others may want nothing to do with working with clients. It is very important to get everyone's input and make your decision as a team. Those members who do not want to work with clients may decide to leave the team, but you could also keep two aspects to your team: those who will work with clients and those who will only be involved with public investigations. Those members that do not want to work directly with clients can also take care of all the background research that will need to be done on the history of the property, the medications the client may be taking, etc. This type of work may also better suit their personality and skills, and you may find that they are the best person on the team for this work. It is all about matching the right people to the right jobs. Not everyone is comfortable or good at talking to people, not everyone is comfortable or good at doing research, and not everyone is good with the technical stuff. Talk with your team members. Find out who enjoys doing what. Get to know them and their personalities. Remember, you will not be successful working and dealing with clients if you cannot work together successfully as a team.

CHAPTER 4
Collecting Client Information

So you and your team have made the big decision to begin conducting client investigations. Now what? How do you go about finding clients to help, and what do you need to know to be able to help them? First, unlike doing investigations of public places or ghost hunting events, you do not go actively looking for clients' properties to investigate. You have to be able to get clients to find you. This means you have to get the existence of your team into the public eye. As every business owner knows—and yes, your team is now becoming a not-for-profit business providing a service—the best way to do this is through a good web presence. A professional looking website that is able to be found on the internet is one of the best starts you can make toward obtaining clients. This may cost you a few dollars, as you will need to buy your domain name (this is the name of your website, e.g., www.spiritsofnewengland.org), a hosting service, and a website design. If you have someone on your team or if you know someone who can build your website, upload it to your hosting site, and maintain it for you, then you can save a lot of money on web design services. In any case, you can expect to spend between three hundred to four hundred dollars to get your website up and running if you design it yourself. Almost all hosting sites provide website design tools when you pay for hosting with them. These tools are typically simple to use, and anyone who is comfortable working with computer programs like PowerPoint® should have no problem using them. I do not recommend using free website hosting services, as you want to present a professional presence to potential clients and having ads pop up all over your website does not present an air of professionalism and confidence to anyone visiting it. Once you have a good website, you may want to think about just how far you are willing to travel to help a client and then focus your efforts in those areas. If your team is in New York, you may just want to focus your investigations within that state and possibly a couple surrounding states; unless your team has unlimited funds and free time, you do not want to be trying to attract clients in California or Canada. Be very clear on your website about what regions of a state, province, or country you provide services to. In any online advertising you might do, limit your advertising range to the areas you service. This will not only help to establish a strong presence in the areas you want to be active in, it will also save you money by not attracting people from areas you do not service. Now that you have a good website and web presence, you can expand it to other social networking sites, such as Facebook® and Twitter®.

So now you have your website up and running and people are checking out your site, but how is a potential client going to contact you? On your website you should create a "contact us" page. At the minimum, you must have a link that any potential client can click on to be able to send you an e-mail. You may also want to provide a phone number that they can reach you at, but *do not* provide your home phone number. If you want to list a phone number, pick up a pay-as-you-go cell phone and list the number for that. You can also list a mailing address if you like, but again, use a post office box. These are all safe and valid ways for clients to be able to contact you.

Let us say you just received your first e-mail or phone call from a potential client and they have provided you some basic information that they believe their house is haunted: they are seeing shadows and hearing voices and footsteps upstairs. They are experiencing cold spots and odd smells from time to time. They have kids who are scared, and they need your help. Now what? Well, it is obvious that the client believes they are experiencing something. But is it really paranormal or something else? The fact is you do not have enough information from them to know for sure what, if anything, is going on. You need details and clarification. You could e-mail them back and forth numerous times to try and gather the information you need; or you could call them, ask them a lot of questions over the phone, and have to write all of their answers down, but you may miss something important in the process. The best way to gather the information you need from your clients is to have a prepared list of questions that you can send to them either by e-mail or regular mail that they can fill out and send back to you. This way it gives the client time to review the questions and provide detailed answers for you and your team. It also gives them a chance to ask you any questions they may have about the form. It provides you and your team with a solid list of valid and relevant questions that will help you figure out what is really going on in the client's property and what you can expect to deal with when you get there. It can also help with figuring out how to approach the investigation, where the hot spots are, and the possible mental and physical condition of the people living there. Now you may be thinking this all sounds great, but how do we get to this point? What type of questions should your team be asking the client? How many questions should you ask? Remember, you need to find out as much information as you can about your client. What is their name, where do they live, how many people live in the property, do they own the property or do they rent an apartment or condo, how long have they lived there, when did their experiences start, and what type of medications, if any, are they on. All of these things are relevant to their case and to your ability to conduct a successful investigation. In the back of this book is a copy of the actual form our team sends to all of our potential clients. It is by no means an all encompassing list of questions, but it does provide us with a very good foundation to work from. It has served us well on all of our investigations. (Feel free to use the form in this book and modify it with your own team name for your use.)

Once the client has completed your form and sent it back to you, make sure to review it with your team. Get everyone's input and feedback on the client's responses. Gather any additional questions your team members have (e.g., Why was a specific question not answered? Was the shadow they saw human shaped or more of a mist?) At this time, you can also decide if your team wants or needs to conduct a preliminary visit to the client's property, or if you just want to set a time and date for the investigation. Once you have done this, it is time to call the client and discuss their answers with them, see what additional information you can gather, and see what questions you can answer for the client. By the end of this phone conversation, you should be able to schedule a date and time with the client for either a preliminary visit, or for the investigation. You have just completed round one of the information gathering phase of your investigation. Round two is about to begin.

So you have the client's completed information, you have gone over it with them, and you have scheduled the date and time for the investigation. Now the day of the investigation has finally arrived, so what should your team do when they first get there? The truth is, there is a lot to do when you first arrive and you need to be organized before you get there. Regardless of the size of your team, each team member should have an assigned task to do and should know what that task is so they can get right to it. At least two of your team members need to meet with the clientand have them take you on a tour of the location. Others on the team should be unloading equipment and getting ready to set up base camp. Once the tour is complete, one of the people who went on the tour should gather the other team members together and go over camera placements and where to set up base camp. Another person should be sitting down with the client and conducting a brief interview with them and any other occupants that may have relevant information for the case. Depending on the size of the location, set up should take anywhere from one to two hours. This will provide plenty of time to interview the client. Another good trick to remember that will help later with review of the case and assist with collecting information from the client is to carry a digital audio recorder—set to continuously record—with you during the client's walk through of the location. I find this much more reliable than walking through with just a notepad and pen taking notes, although that is also good to do for noting best locations for cameras and recorders. The audio recorder will allow you to go back after the investigation is over and confirm information provided on the form and gather any additional details that the client might talk about during the walk through that they did not provide on the initial form. It also makes it easier to note anything odd or unusual that you notice during the walk through, such as the client's DVD collection (perhaps they own lots and lots of paranormal and horror related movies); their book collection; books on witchcraft, the occult, demons, etc.; a Ouija board poking out from under a bed; mold in the bathroom; chipped paint on the walls; overloaded electrical outlets, etc. You can also carry a video camera with you if you prefer to collect visual information along with audio information. Use either a video camera or audio recorder or both when interviewing the client(s); although you may find some clients are not comfortable being videotaped, most do not object to you recording audio of the interview. This again will help you to compare information on the form with that provided during the interview. Are their stories consistent? Did they provide additional information or more details about what they have experienced? Have they had additional experiences since they first contacted you? This is the additional information you are attempting to collect during the interview of the client. Remember, the person interviewing the client should be someone that is open and outgoing, friendly, and easy to talk to. This is the type of person that will get the client to open up in a face-to-face meeting, and this should be the same person they dealt with over the phone. Gathering information from a client is not always an easy thing to do. They do not know you, and you need to have someone on your team who can build a good working relationship with them to gain their trust and get them to open up and give you the information you need to be able to help them. Collecting information on your clients consists of more than just having them fill out a form and talking to them on the phone; it is an ongoing process before, during, and after the investigation.

Another thing to do during the investigation is have your team keep their eyes open for things that might indicate there are others issues at hand, besides just the possibility of something paranormal affecting the client. Look for things that are laying out in the open, such as pill bottles, books and magazines they are reading, notes on the refrigerator about appointments or other things they need to do, photos, DVDs they watch, beer and liquor bottles, and lots of candles, crystals, occult items, etc. Look for how well the home is kept: is it dusty, unkept, cluttered, dirty, etc.? What kind of posters and/or drawings, lists, etc., do the kids put on their walls? Is the house dark or bright inside? All of these things can help you figure out what and why the client may be having odd experiences in their property, be it paranormal in nature or something more natural causing their experiences.

Client investigations are very, very different and much more consequential than investigating a public location, graveyard, or a ghost hunting event. These clients are looking to you for help with something they do not understand. They are looking to you for answers, and by taking their case, you have agreed to help them find those answers. No, you are not getting paid, but you still have an obligation once you accept a client case to do the best you can to help. Look, listen, investigate, review the data, and then, and only then, draw your conclusions and make your recommendations, then report them to the client. There are two quotes from the Sherlock Holmes novels that I think are very significant to this field of work. The first is, "It is a capital mistake to theorize before you have all the evidence. It biases the judgment." The second is, " . . . when you have eliminated the impossible, whatever remains, however improbable, must be the truth."

CHAPTER 5
Conducting an Investigation

At this point, your team has made the decision to work with clients. You have identified each team members' role and their responsibilities on the team. You have been contacted by a client, gathered the detailed information you need from them, and scheduled the investigation date. The day of the investigation is only a week away, so now is the time to begin getting the team prepared to conduct the investigation. I am sure you are wondering why. Why should you start getting ready so soon? What should you be doing to get ready a week before the investigation?

Your case manager should be coordinating with your team leader to determine a time and location for the team to meet before going to the client's home, then contacting all the members of the team and reminding them of the date and time of the investigation, and providing the team with a location, directions, and the time everyone should meet before going to the client's home. You want to make sure that your team shows up at the client's property together. By showing up together it is another way to show your client that your team is organized and professional.

The case manager should also be verifying team member attendance for the investigation. If for some reason one or more team members can't make it, it could have a significant impact on the investigation, or might even mean you need to reschedule the investigation. The team leader or case manager should be providing all team members copies of the client's information form or reminding them to access it and review it again to ensure they are up to date on any new information to make sure it is all fresh in their minds.

The team manager should be identifying specific jobs for team members and then sending out a message to the team with these assignments so everyone knows what their job is for the night of the investigation. It is also the job of the team leader to make sure the case manager is getting these things done.

The technical manager should be making sure all of the investigation equipment is together and in working order. The last thing you want to have happen the night of the investigation is to show up at the client's location and find out your DVR system is not working, or you do not have the power supplies for the cameras, or that you do not have any fresh or fully charged batteries for your audio recorders and video cameras. The technical manager should also be sending out a reminder to all team members to make sure that if they bring any of their own equipment that it is working, they have new batteries in it, and they have extra batteries with them just in case. The team leader may also want to hold a phone conference with everyone a couple days prior to the investigation just to go over the case, the plans for setting up equipment, where the team will meet before going to the client's location, and to address any questions or concerns that any team members might have. These are by no means the only things you can do to get ready, but they are some of the most important to help make sure the investigation goes smoothly.

So the night of the investigation has arrived, and you and your team have arrived at the client's location on time and together. Everyone has their assigned tasks and knows what they are supposed to be doing. The key now to setting up quickly is organization. Even though everyone knows what their task is, you do not want them getting into each other's way trying to accomplish this. I can sum up the key to avoiding this in three words: coordinate, coordinate, coordinate. I can't express the importance of this enough. A well-coordinated team is a successful team.

At this point, the team leader becomes a director. They need to direct the various small teams of one to two individuals. Now is the time to gather everyone in the base camp area and quickly but deliberately go over the task assignment plan with all members of the team. This should be done whether you have a team of ten people or four people to ensure setup goes quickly and smoothly. It helps to have your equipment open and ready to hand out to the team members.

I have personally found that if you are using a DVR system on your investigation, things go much more quickly if you assign at least two to four people—depending on the size of your team—to first run the DVR cables to each room being covered before trying to set up the cameras. This works especially well if you know where you plan to set up the cameras. By doing this, you get the messiest part of setup out of the way first. Then one person can begin taping down the cables while the other person connects the cameras and coordinates camera views with the team member managing the DVR and monitor. This also places team members in separate locations and keeps them from stepping on each other's toes. By using this method, four cameras in a 2,500 square foot home should take about thirty to forty minutes to set up. If you are using mini-DV cameras you can have another team member or the DVR camera person set up these as well. Now that the cameras are setup, the technical manager or assigned team member can now go around and setup an audio recorder in each of the camera locations—at least one with each DVR camera, as mini-DV cameras have their own audio.

You might ask what is the point of this if team members are going to be carrying audio recorders on them for EVP sessions in these locations anyway? The answer to this is simple: maximize your data collection. By putting stationary audio recorders with each DVR camera you maximize your data coverage, increase your chances of capturing EVPs, and can synchronize this audio later with DVR footage to greatly enhance your review process and validate any possible personal experiences that might occur. You can also use this second audio source to help verify or debunk any potential EVPs that you may believe you have captured on a team member's handheld audio recorder in that location.

The last thing the team members can now do is work together to turn off all of the lights throughout the location. Everyone should then return to base camp to begin the investigation.

Okay, you have completed your setup in record time and without any major issues. Now it is time to break up into your predetermined investigative teams and head out to predefined locations. Before leaving base camp, the case manager and team leader should quickly gather the team together to ensure everyone knows where they are going and make sure that each team:

1. Has a walkie-talkie on them.

2. Has an EMF meter, audio recorder, camera, flashlight, extra batteries, and any other equipment that the team leader and team manager have determined is necessary for each investigative team to have.

3. Knows what time the first investigative session is to end and when they are to return to base camp to begin the next session.

4. Has shut off and turned in their cell phones at base camp for the remainder of the investigation.

5. Gives a final safety briefing, reminding everyone to use their flashlights to get to the investigation locations; watch for trip hazards; immediately contact base camp if anyone has a problem or someone gets injured, feels sick, or is just not feeling well; be aware of their surroundings, be professional, be safe, and have fun—after all, even laughter can help encourage a potential spirit in hiding to come out and interact with you.

6. You can also use this brief time to gather any personal experiences that each team member may have had during setup. For this I suggest using an audio recorder to quickly gather everyone's experiences. This will save a lot of time over trying to write them down, and it can easily be reviewed later to accurately report any team member's experiences. This should also be done at the end of the investigation when everything is still fresh in each team member's mind.

Everyone has safely made it to their respective investigation locations. This is where the fun begins. Although I do believe that certain investigative techniques should be used during every client investigation to maintain a control factor, I also believe that each investigator should be allowed and encouraged to use their own investigative methods to add diversity and bring out-of-the-box thinking to the investigation. This is the reason I like conducting at least one-hour sessions at each team's location so that thirty minutes can be spent using the control methods and thirty minutes can be spent freelancing, so to speak. I have found this keeps team members more engaged/interested throughout a long evening. I also believe in conducting multiple investigation sessions of the locations with different team members throughout the night to see if different techniques get different results.

Another productive method I sometimes like to use is to have one investigator sit by themselves in one room while a team of two investigators conduct an EVP session in the room next to them, or a room above or below them. You may be thinking this violates the rule that no investigator should ever be left alone, but that is why I only do this in rooms/locations where we have a DVR camera setup and the single investigator can be monitored from base camp the entire time. The single investigator must also have a working walkie-talkie on them.

I have found that using one investigator as an observer while others are investigating in the room next to them often results in the observer experiencing more activity than the team who is actively investigating. Sometimes having someone just sitting quietly, listening and looking, conducting a static investigation, can be more productive than an active investigation. Why this is I am not sure. Perhaps an entity that might be in the location is curious as to why this person is alone and away from the others. Perhaps it is trying to find a quiet place and is attracted by the fact that this other person also seems to have sought out the same thing. Perhaps it is a bit darker, and is drawn to the seeming vulnerability of this lone individual. This is all just theory and conjecture, but it does seem to get results in a location with real activity. Sometimes the single investigator will witness the activity, but more often than not they will not seem to experience anything; however, upon review of the evidence EVPs will be captured on the recorders in the room, and sometimes even video evidence will be captured on the IR (infrared) camera. Then again, sometimes you get nothing but a very tired and bored investigator, but I still like using this method, especially in a location where the investigators believe they are experiencing activity.

What about using the method of provocation? Well, there is provoking and then there is provoking. I do use provoking as a last resort when I do not feel I am getting anything with other methods, but I *do not use verbal abuse when provoking*. I never swear or make threats at a potential entity/spirit. There are ways to provoke without doing that. How? Talk about the location and how ugly you think their house really is. Remember, it may have been the potential spirit's home at one time. Talk about how rude they are being by not interacting with you after you came so far just to meet them. Tell whomever might be there that you are disgusted with how they have treated you, and you will be telling others how rude they are. Talk about how this will be their only opportunity to speak and interact with you, and once you are gone that is going to be it—they will be alone again forever. Talk about how they are scaring the family or employees that live or work in the location, and how they need to stop doing that, or they are going to have to leave, and that you know how to make them leave unless they talk to you or show themselves to prove they are not a threat to anyone.

These are just some of the ways you can provoke without being completely disrespectful or verbally abusive.

Another good method to use which I have personally had some very good results with is just talking with your other investigator about other investigations you have done, or just talking about friends and family, vacations you have taken, or even just talk gossip. Remember that whatever might be there was probably just a person once. Humans are social beings, and it makes sense that these conversations will attract a potential spirit and possibly trigger interaction with you.

What if you or one of your investigators experiences something they believe to be paranormal, such as hearing a disembodied voice, heavy feelings in a room, unusual EMF readings, cold spots, disembodied footsteps, being touched when no one is near them, feeling scared or as if they should leave the room, or suddenly feeling ill? What should they do? I personally like to initially keep these feelings to myself for a moment to try and verify for myself what is really happening. Did I really see that shadow? Was I really touched, or was it something else? Did I really hear that voice? Then I will ask my investigative partner if they just experienced anything while being very careful not to give away any details to them. I often encourage team members not to contact base camp to report an experience over their walkie, as this can interrupt the other investigative teams, and can also influence the other teams when they investigate that room/location.

I like each team to go in with as little knowledge as possible of what the other team may or may not have experienced. This way, if they experience the same or similar thing, then it validates each team's investigation of that location. Remember, this is a client investigation. You are trying to assist a client with what they are experiencing. To do this you need to try to identify, debunk, verify, and/or validate the possible causes for what your client is experiencing. You need to do this in a controlled manner, with as little external influence as possible. It is human nature to want to tell someone about a unique experience that you had, but try to refrain from doing this during client investigations, at least until the end of the investigation. I feel it is ok for one investigative team to tell another that they did get some activity or had an experience in a particular location, but do not give any details. This way, when you take verbal reports at the end of the investigation, you can see if there were any similar experiences between your teams in the same locations.

On the other side of the coin, if an investigator is overwhelmed by something they have experienced and needs to leave the location, it is extremely important that they try to stay calm. They should tell their investigative partner what they just experienced and that they have to leave the location immediately. Their partner should immediately radio base camp to inform them of the situation and escort their partner back to base camp. *Never* allow a frightened or ill investigator to go back to base camp on their own. Also do what you can to keep them calm and do not allow them to discuss what happened in front of the client. You do not want to possibly scare or upset your client; remember, they live there and may be alone after you leave.

Remember to always follow these simple rules when you experience something that overwhelms you or one of your investigators.

1. Stay calm.
2. Tell your partner.
3. Inform the team.
4. Stay together.
5. Leave the location.
6. Return to base camp.
7. Assess the situation.
8. Do not discuss it in front of the client.

After completing your investigation sessions for the night it is breakdown time. Time to break down your equipment, pack it up, and go home. It is important to remember that even though your entire team is exhausted, you need to be just as professional and organized as when you first arrived and set up. This is important because your client may still be there watching you, and a rushed and disorganized breakdown results in disorganized packing of equipment and even lost equipment, and lost equipment is expensive to replace, especially since you are working for free.

Take your time and double-check that your team has collected all of the equipment. Be diligent in checking the location to make sure nothing was left behind, including personal items. Make sure you leave the location as clean as you found it. Put anything you moved or borrowed from the client back to its original location. Clean up and take with you any trash you may have created (coffee cups, water bottles, snacks, etc.). If the client is there, take a few moments to thank them for their hospitality and let them know when they can expect to hear from you next to set up the reveal with them and go over your findings and report with them. Since it is probably about two or three in the morning by this time, and the client probably has neighbors, leave the location quietly. Do not stand around talking outside, slam your car doors, honk your car horn, etc. Leave quietly and respectfully, and go home and get some rest, because you all still have a lot of work ahead of you to review all the data you just collected.

CHAPTER 6
Reviewing Evidence and Reporting Findings

You have completed the investigation for your client and collected hours and hours of audio and video data, as well as numerous photos and team members' personal experiences. Now it is time to sit down and begin reviewing all of this data. One person cannot do it by themselves, and it has to be done in a timely manner. Remember, this was done for a client; they are looking to you for answers and they want them sooner rather than later. You and your team have an obligation to respond to the client within a reasonable amount of time. Because we are all volunteers in this field of study and we all have full-time jobs, families, and other personal obligations, I always let our clients know that it will be four to six weeks to complete the review of all the data, prepare the report, and then get back to them for the reveal.

I believe this is a reasonable amount of time, given the fact that your team will likely have about fifty to eighty hours of audio and video to review if you ran four DVR cameras, seven audio recorders—one with each DVR camera and one with each of the three investigative teams—and one to two mini-DV cameras, all at approximately four to six hours of data each. It can be a daunting task, and all team members need to pitch in.

So where do you begin? The team leader needs to set a deadline for the completion of all evidence to be reviewed. Personally, I like an initial deadline of three weeks from the day of the investigation and then see how it goes. Each team member who brought their own audio recorder should be responsible for reviewing that audio and providing a report on their findings, along with any Electronic Voice Phenomena (EVP) files, to the team leader and case manager by the deadline date. Their report can be as simple as an e-mail describing what they found, the time location on the original audio file of where the potential EVP is, and the audio file or a clip from the audio file where the EVP is attached to the e-mail. If for some reason a team member does not have a computer, or the computer skills, to be able to accomplish this, then that team member needs to get their audio recorder to a team member or the case manager who can review it for them. Although a team member may be a good investigator, they may need assistance or training with other aspects of the investigative process.

By this time the team as a whole has already decided what team members will be responsible for audio and video review of the team equipment. This typically ends up being the technical manager and assistant technical manager or technical specialist, but even they will need the assistance of other team members to get it all done. Since it may not be practical for the team members to review the data together in one or two days like you see on television shows, you will need an easy way for team members to access the files from various locations at their leisure. There are many good online file storage and sharing websites that make it easy to do this for a reasonable yearly price, or your website hosting company may also be able to provide this service for you. Personally I use MediaFire.com®, which allows me to upload large files and share them with whomever I choose or keep them private. This also allows you to keep your files safely backed up and secure from loss should your personal computer crash for any reason. I also own a backup drive at home, but I am a big believer in backup redundancy; the point here is to be able to easily share files for review among all the team members. The internet is the best and most efficient way to do this.

When it comes to the review of audio, there is a common assumption that just anyone can review audio for EVPs. No one ever seems to ask if the person reviewing the audio has any experience doing it, or if they know what they are listening for. I believe this is a major mistake. It is no different than hiring someone for a job that they have no experience or training for and expecting them to be able to do it right from day one. Would you hire someone to paint your house who had never done it before and expect them to do a professional job?

You want to have the team members with the most experience reviewing the audio. I have also found that some people just seem to have a knack for this, while others struggle with it. EVPs can be tricky things. They can appear as a whispered voice under the voice of an investigator or be just a noise that no one heard at the time. They are not always obvious. There are also different classes of EVPs—Class A, B, and C—and they breakdown as follows:

1. Class A: A very clear voice or noise. Everyone that listens to it hears the same thing.

2. Class B: A voice that can be understood, but not everyone will agree on exactly what is being said—it is obvious that it is a voice, though. Everyone listening to it together will be able to come to a consensus on what is basically being said.

3. Class C: These are the worst quality EVPs. At best it is difficult to determine if it is a voice or a noise. No one who listens to it can determine what is being said.

When working with clients and trying to determine if there is true paranormal activity in a home or business, I prefer to present only Class A or Class B EVPs to them. I also prefer to only present Class B EVPs if there is other evidence captured or experienced at the same time the EVP occurred, such as a personal experience by an investigator, unusual KII meter or Ghost Radar® activity, or something unexplainable caught on camera when the EVP was captured.

I never present a Class C EVP to a client, as I personally believe they are unreliable as potential evidence of paranormal activity.

When reporting findings of potential EVPs to my team I prefer to provide a semi-detailed report, but I do not include what I believe is being said or heard. This way I do not bias the review of the other team members. Here is an example of my reporting of an actual EVP that was captured during one of our investigations.

DWH_Attic2_20101211_TS05439-RecdrB: There are two potential EVPs that appear between approximately 11.4 sec and 15.1 sec into the file. There is no one in the attic at this time. Investigator Sarah had left the attic just moments before these potential EVPs were captured. Prior to this she had been talking about the guns downstairs and about her grandfather's guns.

Notice the first designations of the file name: these identify the file information. DWH stands for the place being investigated (Deane Winthrop House). The next identifies the location in the house and the investigative session (Attic Session 2). The next line identifies the date of the investigation

(Year-2010, Month-12, Day-11). The next line identifies the time on the original audio file that the EVP occurred (Time Stamp 05439 = 0 hours, 54 minutes, 39 seconds into the original audio file). The next line identifies the audio recorder on which the EVP was captured (Recorder B). This information can be used to check it against video data or other audio data to see what was happening at the time and if it is an actual EVP, or perhaps one of the investigators.

The next part of the report identifies where in the file the potential EVPs appear. The next lines describe what was going on at the time the EVPs were captured. I do not tell what I believe I heard so as not to bias the other team members when they listen to the file, although I do keep a separate version of the report where I do identify what I believe I heard. This way, after everyone else e-mails back their findings, we can compare them and see what the consensus is, even if that consensus is that the voice is one of our own investigators. In any case, this is just one way of reporting. The point here is to find a good way of reporting that works for your team and gives enough detail without biasing the review by the rest of the team.

Once your EVP report is complete you can send it out to the rest of the team, along with the EVPs, and get a consensus from everyone on what they believe they hear and if it is an EVP at all. Sometimes what we believe may be an EVP can turn out to be one of the investigators whispering, or even outside contamination that occurred during the investigation. One of the other investigators may remember the event and be able to positively identify what the possible voice or noise is. This is why it is extremely important for all members of the investigation team to review the audio and provide their feedback in a timely manner. You do not want to go into the reveal with the client, present what you believe is an EVP, and then have one of your team members say, "Oh, that is not an EVP, that was me whispering in the background." This makes you look very unprofessional and unorganized in the eyes of a client, not to mention how embarrassing it can be to all involved.

Video evidence is just as important as audio evidence, and must be reviewed just as thoroughly. Again, it is very important to label your files accurately with the location name, area of the location where the video was filmed, date of the investigation, time the event was captured, and the camera that recorded the event. This information is critical to the data collection and review process to identify what was happening at the time the event was captured and where everyone was at the time. Unlike audio evidence, video evidence can be much more subtle, and more difficult to identify. I guarantee you are not going to see a fully formed ghost go floating across the screen in front of your camera. Yes, this type of evidence does happen every once in a blue moon, such as the occasional piece of footage that you may have seen on paranormal television shows, but this is atypical. Typical paranormal video evidence is just never that obvious. It is often very subtle, such as a shadow moving in the background that just does not make sense with what else is happening in the area, or it can be an odd, bright light that just appears out of nowhere, lingers for a moment, and then disappears. It may even be something less obvious, such as a black mass that appears on the video for only a moment while you are panning from one section of a room to another but was not seen by the investigator at the time. It could also be as simple as something in the shot moving slowly over a few minutes time, such as a lamp or a chair. This would not be noticed at the time by the investigators but will be more obvious on video. It could also be more obvious, like a door opening or closing; in either of these cases there will be no visible source making the item move. The point here is that you need to be vigilant in your review of video footage and look for anything that just does not fit or does not make sense.

Once you think you have found something that could be evidence you need to try to find a reason for it. Watch more of the video after the activity to make sure that what you found is not being caused by one of the investigators or something else more natural. Double check the footage before the activity for the same reason. Once you are pretty sure this might be something paranormal review it with the rest of the team to see if anyone remembers this moment in the investigation and see if they know what may have caused the activity. Whether its audio, video, or another type of evidence, you always need to have the investigative team review it to get a consensus.

Other evidence that needs to be gathered and reviewed is the personal experiences of each of the investigators from the night of the investigation. I find the best and quickest way to do this is to have each investigator submit an e-mail report within one or two days after the investigation so that it is still fresh in their minds. These reports are just simple two or three paragraph e-mails about their experiences that night. These can then be reviewed later by the team member putting the final report together so that they can add anything of importance to the final report. Another great way to review the personal experiences of the investigators is to review the audio files from the digital recorders that were used that night. This will be your best documentation of any personal experiences that occurred that night, as typically whenever an investigator does have a personal experience, they will discuss what they just experienced with the team member they are investigating with and it will be captured on the audio file. Remember that I discussed how I like to have each team member give a quick audio interview during the investigation, either during a break or before everyone leaves for the night, of any experiences they may have had during the investigation. If you did this, then these audio files can also be reviewed.

The last thing that needs to be done is to research the history of the home and surrounding area, not just to see if there are deaths associated with the home, business, or location, but to also see what type of geology, water sources, electrical sources, and even seismic earthquake data exists in the area. Someone on the team needs to be assigned to do this research as well. Much of this information can be found on the internet, but some of it will require phone calls to the local historical society, a visit to the local library, and even a visit to the local city/county clerk's office where the home/business is located. This is not an easy task, and in many ways is the most difficult task of the entire review process. It can also end up being the most important information you will gather.

Now that the audio, video, personal experiences, and historical evidence review is completed and you have a consensus from the team on all of it, you will want to forward your preliminary reports to the person on the team that will be putting together the final report for the client. This person will now have the job of putting all the evidence, personal experiences, and historical information together in a report form that is detailed, organized, and easy to understand. The individual writing the report will also have the task of identifying and putting together multiple events that occurred during the investigation. What I mean by this is that this person, in writing the report, will need to review all of the evidence and identify any individual events that may have occurred at the same time, such as an EVP captured at the same moment that an investigator had a personal experience and at that same time there was a hit on a KII meter, or another investigator also had an experience at the same time but in another location. It is this type of multiple activities at the same time that gives you the strongest evidence of paranormal activity. These are the type of things that the person preparing the report wants to look for and include in the report.

Here is the organizational method for a report that I personally like to use:

1. Investigation Location: Where you investigated, including the address.

2. Date of the Investigation: The date of the actual investigation.

3. Report Prepared By: Who wrote the report and their team title.

4. Reported To: The client whom the report is being prepared for.

5. Background: Details of the background of the case, who initially contacted the team, what the client's claims of activity were, when the activity began, and what the client believes is the cause of the activity they are experiencing.

6. History of the Home/Business and Surrounding Area: When the home or business was built, who was the original owner, are there any deaths associated with it, what is the geology of the area, what is the history of seismic activity, are there any nearby water sources (rivers, lakes, etc.), and what other facts/points of history were found that may be relevant to the case. In this section you may also want to include photos of the location and maps of the area identifying relevant aspects in relation to the location, such as rivers, lakes, cemeteries, etc.

7. Client Background: This section should include all of the information that the client provided about themselves from the original client information form they provided, as well as information from any interviews that were conducted with the client. Information here should include medical history, current medical condition, history of drug and/or alcohol use if any, religious beliefs, client's age, current medications, details of activity and experiences reported by the client, and any other information that is relevant to the case.

8. Investigation Details and Findings: This section should include the sequence of events and details of the investigation from the night it took place, including what time the team arrived, who they were greeted by, and the results of the EMF sweep of the home/business.

Include details on any problems that were found and the average EMF level of each room. It should also include a room by room breakdown of the night's investigation and what was experienced in each room, including any EVPs that were captured, personal experiences, video evidence, etc. This should also include the details and results of any debunking that was done and what was discovered.

This section may also include any relevant photos showing individual rooms and identifying where activity was experienced, items in the rooms that may be causing or giving off high EMF levels, and anything that the team may feel is relevant to the case that will be helpful to the client to see. This section will be the bulk of the report.

9. Conclusions and Recommendations: This section is where you wrap up the report. You will identify for the client any issues or problems you found with the home that may be causing some or all of the activity that the client is experiencing, including high EMF levels, the existence of rodents in the home/business, issues with mold in the home, issues with chemicals in the home, etc.

This section should also include information on the medical affects that these things can have on an individual. This section will also include the team's assessment of any possible paranormal aspects to this case and any recommendations the team has for dealing with this, and/or if this paranormal activity is anything that the client should be concerned with, or if it is something that just exists in the location but poses no threat or concern to the client.

You can also view a copy of one of our S.P.I.R.I.T.S. team's actual client investigation reports on our website at http://www.spiritsofnewengland.org/investigations.html. These reports do not include any personal information on our clients, but they will give you a very good idea of how to prepare a good, detailed investigation report for a client.

Now that you have completed the investigation report it needs to be reviewed by the team for accuracy and final approval by the team founder(s) before it is presented to the client. The quickest way to do this is to e-mail it to the team or upload it to the same location/website on the internet that you share all of the EVPs and video files with the team. I like to set a deadline of one week to allow the team to review the report.

You want to get this done quickly, as you want to have the reveal with the client and get this information to them as soon as possible. The best way to allow team members to comment on the report is by e-mail. If they notice anything wrong they can e-mail you their comments and you can then go back and revise the report.

You should *always* include in the report file name the revision letter of the report. I like to start with revision "New" and then go from there, so the original report name might be something like, "Client Home Investigation-Rev-New." Any changes to the original report would then be identified with a new letter designation (A, B, C, etc.), so the second revision would be, "Client Home Investigation-Rev-A," and so on. Once you complete the review and approval of the report then you are ready to set up the reveal with the client and hopefully give them the answers they have been searching for.

It is now your case manager's turn to contact the client and set up a date and time with the client for the reveal. Prior to this the team members that will be involved with the reveal—usually only two or three members—should have agreed on a few dates within the next two weeks that they are available. The case manager should contact the client with these options and see which date and time is best for them. Once this date and time is confirmed, the case manager needs to e-mail the members involved to confirm this. The case manager should also make a follow-up call to the client a day or two before the meeting to re-confirm. At this point, at least two copies of the report should be made: one for the team and one for the client. A CD should also be made that includes a copy of the report and any EVPs and video evidence that will be shown to the client during the reveal, so that this CD can be given to the client for them to keep for their own records.

Once the date for the reveal comes, just as with the investigation, be sure to be on time for your appointment with the client. This again shows your professionalism and reliability as a team. While doing the reveal to the client, it is very important to keep the clients' feelings and emotional state in mind. I often find that most clients already have it set in their mind that their home is haunted, whether it is or not, and they almost always seem to feel it is either demonic or a family member that is watching over them. Typically what we find as paranormal teams completely contradicts clients' beliefs, or in some cases the client is hoping that there is nothing living in their home or business with them and you may have to report to them that there is something. In either case, you have to watch and maintain awareness of how the client is reacting to the information you are revealing to them and be able to help them cope with it.

Yes, you have to help them cope with it. This is your team's responsibility to the client. No matter what you have found during the investigation, you have the responsibility to provide the client with assistance to deal with these findings and try to help them resolve these issues by providing them with knowledge and perhaps even some suggestions of where to go next. For instance, if part of your findings is that they have high EMF levels throughout their entire home, which is what may be giving them the feeling that they are sick, headaches, the feeling that they are being watched, etc., you may want to give them a recommendation to have an electrician come in and inspect their home, and perhaps fix the wiring. If you find that they are experiencing paranormal activity in their home, and even though you have assured them that it is not harmful, they may still want to have you get rid of it for them. This may be beyond what your team is able to do, so you may want to have information on a reliable and responsible psychic medium that can do a house cleansing for them. You may find that some of the experiences they are having are due to the medications they are taking, and in this case you need to suggest they discuss these side effects with their doctor. By having printouts of the side effects of their medications with you it can make it easier for the client to accept the fact that their experiences are not anything paranormal. Again, the point here is to be aware of your client's feelings and emotions and work with them to help them resolve the problems/issues you have discovered during your investigation—paranormal or otherwise—and make it clear to them that you are still there to assist them if they need you, even after the reveal is over. Our team has been working with clients for many years and we still have some clients that contact us to this day just to talk about their case and new things that are going on with them. Remember, your client came to you because they did not understand what they were experiencing and they did not know where else to turn for help. They may still feel that way months or even years after you did the investigation for them, especially if you foundd evidence of paranormal activity.

Working with clients is a complex and complicated piece of the paranormal investigation process. It requires a high level of dedication to the field of paranormal research and to the clients involved. It is difficult and time consuming work, and it is not for everyone, nor for every team. For those that choose this path, it can be the most rewarding work there is in the field of paranormal research.

CHAPTER 7

Equipment

Ghost hunting equipment, paranormal tools, ghost gear, or scientific equipment for paranormal investigating; no matter how you phrase it or what you call it, when it all comes down to it, there is no such thing as ghost hunting gear. It simply does not exist. None of the equipment or tools that we use for investigating the paranormal was ever truly designed for that purpose. There is no equipment on the market today that can detect a ghost, and neither is there ever likely to be any such equipment anytime soon. You may think I am wrong, and you may even think that you know of at least one piece of electronic equipment that was designed specifically for ghost hunting. While that statement may be true, and I will concede that point, none of the equipment you are thinking of, such as the Mel Meter, Spirit Box, KII, E-Pods, REM-Pods, RT-EVP, full spectrum cameras, IR cameras, or any one of numerous other pieces of electronic equipment or cameras, can identify the presence of a ghost. What they can do—at least a few of them—is detect changes in the environment, identify sources of EMF, record sound levels that cannot be heard by the human ear, and photograph visual spectrums we cannot physically see. Others are just paper weights or dust collectors, and not any use at all for investigating the paranormal. What I intend and hope to do here is educate you on the different types of equipment on the market today that purport to be designed for paranormal investigating, what they are actually designed to do, and whether or not they are worth their salt at all for our field of work.

The Digital Audio Recorder

This is actually the number one of my top three picks for equipment that every paranormal investigator must have in their tool box. To be honest, the audio recorder is *the* most important piece of equipment a paranormal investigator needs to have, because the majority of tangible paranormal evidence you will collect will be Electronic Voice Phenomena (EVP). In case you are new to the paranormal community, an EVP is a spirit voice that is captured on either a digital audio recorder or an analog audio recorder—in other words, audio tape. These are voices that were not heard by investigators at the time they were captured on the audio recorder. Given the importance of this piece of equipment and audio evidence, you want to make sure that the audio recorder you purchase is of very good quality. The more serious you are about investigating the paranormal, the more you have to be willing to invest in high quality equipment. Having said that, I understand that even those of us committed to paranormal research can't always afford the best quality equipment available on the market, but we can get very high quality audio recorders that will hurt our wallet a little but not wipe out our bank account.

Those of you who are new to the paranormal field, paranormal enthusiasts, or just want to go on an occasional ghost hunting event, you can also purchase a decent quality recorder at a reasonable price. So how do you know a quality recorder from one that is only good as a paperweight? The following is what you need to look for in a quality audio recorder regardless of your level of paranormal investigating:

1. Microphone: When discussing microphones as off-the-shelf, handheld, digital audio recorders, this is a simple choice of mono or stereo: one channel recording or two channel recording. Even as a beginner or enthusiast, I strongly recommend choosing a recorder with a stereo microphone, as it will help capture a much better quality recording and increase your chances of capturing and then finding potential EVPs when reviewing your audio because of the better quality stereo sound you get during playback.

2. Recording Format, Mode, and Frequency Response: Although it may seem like I am bundling three separate items in one, when it comes to digital audio recorders, they are actually all directly linked to each other. Most information provided by manufacturers only points out the device's recording formats (MP3, WMA, or WAV) and modes (48, 128, 192, and sometimes even 320 kbps for MP3 format; LP, SP, HQ, ST HQ, or ST XQ for WMA format; and 8000 Hz - 16 bit, 16000 Hz - 16 bit, 24000 Hz - 16 bit, 32000 Hz - 16 bit, 44100 Hz - 16 bit, or 48000 Hz - 16 Bit for WAV format). There are also 8 bit recording modes for each of the Hz frequencies listed for WAV format, but it is always best to record in the larger 16 bit file size. The normal/default WAV format setting is 44100 Hz - 16 bit, which is a CD quality recording that I recommend using for EVP work.

Recording formats have a direct impact on the frequency response of the recording. Why is this so important? Because both of these directly impact the quality of the audio recording and the frequency range in which the recording is made. These two things directly impact your chances of capturing EVPs. Almost all digital audio recorders provide two MP3 recording modes: Moving Picture Experts Group (MPEG) and Windows Media Audio (WMA). Both of these formats are compression formats, meaning that when you are recording your audio, it will be compressed by the format and mode you choose to record in. I am not going to get into the details of what file compression does, except to say that when it comes to recording audio for capturing EVPs, file compression is *not good*. Since almost all low- to mid-priced digital recorders come with only MP3 and WMA recording options you really cannot get away from file compression, unless you are willing to spend more money on a higher end digital audio recorder that records in uncompressed WAV format. What you can do to ensure you get the highest quality sound recording possible at a price that will not empty your wallet is look for a recorder which can record in WMA format with a recording mode of at least Stereo High Quality (ST HQ) and/or MP3 format with a recording mode of at least 192 kbps. Regardless of the recording format you prefer, by using the highest quality recording settings available, you will greatly improve your chances of capturing EVPs and being able to hear them clearly when reviewing your audio.

3. Internal Memory Storage (Flash Memory): Because you want to be
recording in a format and mode that generates large files, you want
a digital recorder that has a large internal memory storage capacity,
also called flash memory. Most manufacturers advertise how many
hours their recorders can record (i.e., 131 hours, 536 hours, 1151
hours), but it is very important to note that these advertised hours are
estimated at the lowest quality recording settings, e.g., MP3 format at
48 kbps or WMA format in LP mode. Still, a recorder that advertises
to be able to record 800 hours of audio at these lowest recording
settings will still be able to record up to eight or nine hours at the
higher settings (MP3 format at 192 kbps or WMA format in ST HQ
mode). This is more than enough hours of recording time for a long
night of investigating. If you want to transfer these advertised hours
into memory size, that can be a bit difficult to do because of the large
variation in recording hours from manufacturer to manufacturer
and recorder to recorder. So to make it simple, if you want to look
at memory size/capacity, I would just look for a recorder that has
either 1 GB or 2 GB of memory. Either of these is more than enough
memory for a full six to eight hours of investigation. I personally have
four recorders that each have 1GB of memory, and I set each of them
up to record with one of our DVR cameras all night (six to seven
hours) during an investigation in WMA format in ST HQ mode, and
even after that many hours I still have memory left on the recorders.
I once let one of these record all night during an investigation and
it ran for over nine hours before running out of memory. The nice
thing about the new digital recorders is that you usually need to
worry about running out of memory before you have to worry about
changing out batteries, and thank heavens we do not have to worry
about dealing with cassette tapes anymore. Most recorders will claim
to run for a full fifty to seventy hours before you need to change the
batteries, but I typically find that they will run for at least twelve
to fifteen hours before the batteries die. It is important to note that
temperature has a big impact on battery life: the colder it is, the
shorter the life batteries have. This is most likely one reason why we
paranormal investigators go through so many batteries, as we always
seem to be investigating locations that are unheated, cold, and damp.
The good news is that all the digital recorders today seem to run on

triple-A batteries, so those will not cost you an arm and a leg, either. The exception to this is the higher end digital recorders, such as the Zoom family (H2, H4, H4n, etc.), that use double-A batteries, but can also be run on their AC adapter.

4. USB Port: Since you will want to be able to download your files from your digital recorder to your computer to best review them using audio software, or even just to move them from your recorder to your computer to free up space for your next investigation without having to delete files, it is extremely important to purchase a digital audio recorder that has either a USB port or a USB plug. This comes as a standard option on most digital recorders, but there are still some out there that do not, so you want to be sure to read the specifications on the package before purchasing to make sure the recorder has a USB connection. Sometimes what looks like a good buy on a digital recorder is priced that way because it does not have a USB port, so everything that you record on it stays on it unless you delete it. As a paranormal investigator in today's environment, a digital audio recorder with no USB port is useless if I cannot get the files off the recorder to review them in an audio software program, where I can pull out audio clips of what I believe to be potential EVPs so that I can listen to them in more depth later on, or boost the audio if necessary to better hear the EVPs without modifying the original file. This also allows me to e-mail any EVPs to other team members for their review, and also put them on a CD to give to a client at a reveal, or to just save those great EVPs in smaller files to be able to quickly pull up and play back for friends who are interested and want to hear them.

5. Microphone Sensitivity: All good quality digital audio recorders have a setting for microphone sensitivity. The ones that do not have only one setting built into the recorder set by the manufacturer. Since there is no way of knowing for sure exactly what this setting is, you want to look for a recorder that has a microphone sensitivity setting option. With some recorders, this can be an external switch on the side of the recorder that allows for a choice of up to three option modes, such as Lecture, Conference, or Dictation. Others have

option modes on the internal electronic menu of High or Low. When recording for EVPs, you want to use the microphone sensitivity mode that allows the microphone to pick up as much of the audio spectrum as possible. In a recorder with a High or Low setting you want to set the microphone sensitivity to High. In a recorder with the Lecture, Conference, or Dictation options you want to set your recorder to Conference mode, as this is the highest sensitivity setting the microphone has. High sensitivity means that no ambient noise or sounds are being filtered out by the microphone. Again, when trying to capture EVPs, you do not want to filter any sound from your recordings.

These are the five most important things you want to look for when choosing a digital audio recorder, as well as how to use them and their impact on recording for EVPs. I know what you are thinking: While all this information is good, what brand should I buy? Who makes the best recorders for my money? While I did not really want to get into brands and models because they change so often as much as what is important to look for, I can give you my personal top rankings for quality digital audio recorders that will not break the bank:

1. Olympus Model DM-620: This one may have a few extra functions that you do not really need for paranormal investigation, such as an expandable memory card slot, but the high quality TRESMIC 3 stereo microphone system makes it worth the price for the serious paranormal investigator.

2. Olympus Model WS-700M: This one is a great investment for the seasoned or serious investigator. It has all five of the recommended requirements and a 4 GB internal flash memory for extended recording time.

3. Olympus Model WS-600S: If there is any recorder out there that exactly meets my five requirements for a quality audio recorder for paranormal investigating this is the one. It has everything the seasoned to beginner investigator needs to capture quality recordings and easily download their files for review at a very reasonable price.

4. Olympus Model VN-8100PC: This is actually an excellent little recorder for the beginning investigator or paranormal enthusiast. The only drawback is that it does not have a built-in stereo microphone, but it does have a microphone input where you can plug in a separate external mic. This allows you to upgrade the recorder to a better microphone later on if you so desire. I actually own this recorder, and have used it on many investigations as a stand-alone recorder set up with a DVR camera to capture audio during an entire night's investigation. It has worked out very well, and I have captured several Class A and B EVPs with it.

I am sure you have noticed that my first four recommendations are all Olympus recorders. This is because Olympus manufactures a high quality, durable, and reliable recorder. The sound quality they produce is excellent, even with the lower cost models. I own five of their recorders and have accidently dropped more than one of them from at least four to five feet on more than one occasion, and they still perform as if nothing ever happened. The menu functions are easy to access and figure out, and the record, stop, play, and volume buttons are always easy to find and use. With that said, I can also recommend the following Sony brand recorders:

1. Sony Model ICDSX712: There are a couple of reasons I like and recommend this recorder, especially for the serious investigator. It can record in PCM and WAV format; I like the two-position adjustable stereo microphone, which enhances your ability to capture high quality stereo audio recordings; and I like the microSD card capability for expanding memory. I also really like the price, given the advanced functions this recorder has to offer.

2. Sony Model ICDUX512: This is another excellent recorder for the seasoned and/or serious investigator. Again, I like this one for its ability to record in PCM and WAV format for recording uncompressed audio and stereo sound. It also has the ability, like the Sony ICDSX712, to accept a microSD card for expanded memory storage.

3. Sony Model ICDAX412: This is the last of the Sony recorders I would recommend, even for the beginning investigator or paranormal enthusiast. It has all of the five qualities that are necessary, it has the microSD card memory expansion option, and the price is very reasonable.

If you want to invest in a much higher end digital audio recorder, I would recommend one of the following:

1. Zoom H4 Handy Portable Digital Recorder: High quality built-in X/Y stereo microphones, better-than-CD quality recording capability, large memory (32 GB), and the ability to run on AC power or double-A batteries make this well worth the price for the seasoned or serious paranormal investigator.

2. Zoom H2 Handy Portable Digital Recorder: This is another great recorder for the seasoned or serious investigator. The 360-degree sound recording in CD quality on two or four channels makes this a great advanced recorder. Not only can you capture the highest quality recordings, but you can also use the software that is included to tell what direction a sound or voice is coming from.

3. RT-EVP Digital Recorder and Spirit Box: This is currently the only digital recorder designed and built by a paranormal investigator for paranormal investigators. Although it does not meet all of the five requirements I have defined, it does record in WAV format, and of course has the great function to be able to listen to your recording in real time while you are recording. You can set it up with anything from a one- to sixty-second delay. The advantage of this is that if you do capture an EVP, you will hear it within seconds after it is captured, which may allow you to respond to it. The other great function of this device is the built in spirit box, so it is actually two devices in one; you can also record your spirit box session on the device while performing it so you can review it later and save any potential evidence you might have captured. It also has an 8 GB memory, which is very helpful, given the large file sizes that are created with the higher quality recording modes it has. This is a fairly complicated device, so I really only

recommend it for the serious/experienced paranormal investigator. I personally used this device during several investigations and had some very interesting results using the built in spirit box function and also being able to hear EVPs as they were captured, which allowed us to ask potentially more relevant questions during our EVP sessions.*

So if the digital audio recorder is the most important piece of equipment in the paranormal investigator's arsenal, just as important and directly related to the audio recorder is the audio editing software you should use to review your recordings. While it is true you can just review your audio right on the recorder itself, this will not allow you to pull out audio clips of potential EVPs, or, if necessary, clean up the audio of those potential EVPs to hear them more clearly. To do that you will need to download the original audio files to your computer and play them back through some type of audio software.

Digital Audio Editing Software

Software is not exactly equipment, but it is a very important tool for the paranormal investigator. It goes hand in hand with your digital audio recorder when it comes to reviewing your audio files for EVPs. Although your new audio recorder will come with its own software, it is very limited in what it can do, and the quality and type of filters it has, such as volume amplify and noise reduction, are limited or nonexistent. So what other types of audio software are there and where can you get them? There are numerous audio editing software packages available, and all of them are available on the internet, but which ones are right for doing EVP work? Even more important, what do you really need to look for in an audio editing program for EVP review?

The important thing to remember as a paranormal investigator is that you do not want to do too much editing to your audio. When it comes to EVPs, the less editing you do the better. At times you may want to try and clean up an audio file to be able to better hear an EVP. To do this, you will need a program that has filters that allow you to enhance the audio by removing background noise, such as hiss and pop, and amplify the audio. This is all that I will do when it comes to editing EVP files; when possible, I will not do anything at all to them, or I will at most just amplify the audio.

* Some recorders may no longer be available from the manufacturer or have newer models; they may still be available online from third party sellers. The important thing is to look for an audio recorder that meets the five recommended requirements.)

At this point you may be asking: If the audio program that came with my recorder has these filters then why do I need another program? Because the quality of the filters you will use vary greatly from program to program. The programs that come with your recorder are very simple and the filters that come with them are not of great quality. This will significantly affect the sound and results you get with an EVP when you edit, and in some cases the filters you apply to your EVP can even distort it. There are some very good programs on the internet that have excellent editing filters, and the programs are either free, or their professional versions are very reasonably priced. Probably the best audio editing program is Adobe Audition®—it is an extremely powerful and high quality audio editing program, but it is also expensive. Adobe® does provide a free thirty-day trial of the program so you can decide if it is right for you. Audition® is far more than the paranormal investigator needs for EVP work, and in our case not worth the money.

There are several other programs that are worth the expense for the professional versions if you are a seasoned or serious investigator, but the beginning investigator or paranormal enthusiast will be more than pleased with the results and functions of the free versions. Here are the audio editing programs I recommend for EVP work:

1. WavePad Sound Editor © NCH Software (free version and Master's Edition available): After trying several other free programs and even the free trial of Adobe Audition®, I found WavePad Sound Editor to be my personal choice for EVP work. This program has a user-friendly interface, the filters are of high quality, and the program is reliable and stable. Creating audio clips from the master audio file is easy. I prefer to save clips of the audio sections where I find a potential EVP so that I can edit the clip file and leave the original file unedited. The free version of WavePad provides the two basic editing filters you need for EVP work: Amplify Audio and Noise Reduction. The Master's Edition provides these and much more, but the ones I use the most in the Master's Edition for EVP work are Amplify Audio, High-Pass Filter, and Speed Change. The ability to have the use of the last two filters was well worth the cost of the program.

2. Dexster Audio Editor by SoftdivSD Software (free version and full version available): The free version of this software is adequate

for EVP work, but the full version has many more useful filters. The program is very user-friendly and easy to navigate. I do not like this software as much as WavePad, only because WavePad has more advanced features than Dexster, and is thus more useful to me for the amount of EVP work I do. Dexster Audio Editor is very good for those looking for an easy-to-use audio editing program for reviewing and editing their audio.

3. GoldWave Digital Audio Editor by GoldWave Inc. (free version and full version available): Like Dexster, this program has a very user-friendly interface. It does lack some filters and tools, but they may be a bit complicated for someone who has never used an audio editing program before. The full version does give you a few filters you may want to use for enhancing your EVPs.

4. Audacity® by the Audacity Team (free software): Audacity is a fully free program; it was the first audio editing program I ever used for EVP work. It is a great program for the beginner and paranormal enthusiast, as it is very easy to use, has good filters and tools, and it is completely free. The filters are not as high quality as Dexster or WavePad, but they are adequate. This is a great audio program to learn to use audio editing before moving on to a more advanced one. I strongly recommend this one to those just starting out in the paranormal field and the enthusiast.

Some of the most popular pieces of equipment said to be designed specifically for the paranormal investigator, specifically Mel Meters and E-Pods, were both designed by Gary Galka, president of DAS Distribution, the same man that developed the very useful RT-EVP digital audio recorder.

The Mel Meter

The Mel Meter has come a long way since its first incarnation (the Mel Meter 8704). The 8704 was, and still is, a great development for assisting the paranormal investigator. It combines an EMF meter with an ambient temperature gauge, and a follow-up revision even includes a built in flashlight, which is the model I personally own. The backlit digital readout screen is also a great help for investigators, who are almost always working in the dark. The best thing about this device is that it combines multiple pieces of equipment into one compact device at a price that is much less expensive than having to buy an EMF meter, temperature gauge, and flashlight separately. It not only saves having to purchase multiple pieces of equipment, but also helps save a lot of money on batteries. The single nine-volt battery it takes is also a great design choice given the multiple functions of the device, providing plenty of power and long life. The additional functions provided, such as the record function to be able to record and review the maximum and minimum EMF and temperatures measured by the device, the ability to turn the backlight on and off to either extend the battery life or just go completely dark in a location, the ability to change the range of the EMF readout or change the units that the EMF is read in (mGauss or uTesla) all make the Mel Meter a great electronic device for not only paranormal research, but also electricians, scientists, and engineers.

Multiple models are now available. These newer models include various additional functions, such as an integrated KII and an Extremely Low Frequency (ELF) EM field range down to 30Hz. This is a great addition, as it allows for electromagnetic measurements in the lower bandwidth 30Hz up to 50Hz, which other standard EMF detectors and KII units do not provide. Glowing buttons allow the investigator to see the buttons on the device in the dark. They also have Natural Field Detection to identify natural EMF, an EMF Radiating Antenna, a Hot and Cold Spot Alarm, and much more. One of the newest models, the Mel-8704R-SB7 even incorporates the SB7 Spirit Box.

All of the model variations, as well as the original Mel-8704, provide the paranormal investigator with a wide variety of equipment functions compacted into one easy-to-carry and easy-to-use device. This device was definitely designed for the paranormal investigator, but it is important to remember that this device, as well as all other devices currently being used for paranormal research, is *not* designed to find or identify ghosts. The Mel Meter is designed to identify electromagnetic fields and ambient temperature changes, which are two of the variables that are at the core of current scientific paranormal research and investigation.

The Mel Meter provides a great advantage over other off-the-shelf EMF meters and temperature gauges that are popular with paranormal investigators, as it provides great functionality for working in the dark. It is this combination of functions provided into one reasonably priced device that makes the Mel Meter a great piece of equipment for the paranormal investigator, and it is well worth the financial investment. If you are new to the paranormal field or a paranormal enthusiast, I recommend either the Mel-8704R-EMF or the Mel-8704R-ProNavigator EMF. Both of these provide the great combination of EMF detector and ambient temperature measurement, along with a flashlight and other functions, at a very reasonable cost. If you are a seasoned or serious investigator, then I would recommend any one of the upper end models, such as the Mel-8704R-KII Hybrid up to the Mel-8704R-SB7 Spirit Box model. You can get some great detailed information on all of these Mel Meter variations at DAS Distribution's website (http://www.dasdistribution.com/products/) or at http://www.pro-measure.com (Pro-Measure is a division of DAS Distribution). Both of these websites provide a good amount of detail on all of their products, and they even have great videos on how to use the equipment, as well as links to other paranormal websites that give their own evaluations of the products.

Closed-Circuit Television Digital Video Recorders (CCTV DVR)

There are very few paranormal teams that do not use a CCTV DVR security system for their investigations, and why not? These systems offer a great advantage to any team during an investigation. In the simplest way, it adds more investigators to the team through the number of cameras the system has.

Although most of us think of CCTV systems as new technology, it was actually invented by German engineer Walter Bruch in 1942, for the purpose of observing the launch of V-2 rockets. The first commercial CCTV system became available in the United States in 1949. It was not until videocassette recorder (VCR) technology—providing the ability to record and erase information—became commercially available in the 1970s that CCTV surveillance systems became more common in businesses. At that time these systems were still rather expensive and not widely affordable. The 1980s saw a real surge in the use of these security systems when law enforcement across the country began to utilize CCTV surveillance systems in public areas, as it was seen as a cheap way to deter crime over hiring more police officers. Also many twenty-four hour stores and gas stations in high crime areas installed CCTV systems to help deter crime.

During the 1990s, the advent of the digital age made it easy and affordable for just about anyone to own and install a CCTV system to monitor their businesses and homes. Advances in digital technology allowed for an owner of one of these systems to run multiple cameras and record the data to a single recording system knows as a DVR (Digital Video Recorder), which replaced the VCR and all of its bulky magnetic tape videocassettes. Prior to the DVR, an owner would have to have one VCR for each CCTV camera they were running if they wanted to record from the camera; otherwise, the user would have to have someone checking the CCTV on a monitor. CCTV and DVR technology made huge advancements throughout the 1990s and into the twenty-first century. CCTV cameras now have much improved video resolution—even in infrared (IR) mode—they switch between day and night modes automatically, and depending on the number of CCTV cameras being operated and the size of the hard drive in the DVR, they can record hundreds of hours of video. Some cameras now even have built in audio recording. The standard CCTV camera can now see out to thirty feet in IR (night vision) mode. There are even wireless CCTV DVR systems available so you do not have to run hundreds of feet of cable from each camera back to the DVR recorder. Two of the biggest advancements in these systems in the last few years are the software improvements that now allow the owner to monitor their CCTV system right from their computer or smartphone and the significant drop in the cost of these systems, which has made them affordable to just about everyone. Now we see them used just about everywhere, and can even watch live streaming video through the use of CCTV (i.e., webcams) of your favorite vacation spots or Skype® with your friends—yes, even your computer's webcam is just a version of a CCTV camera.

DVR Systems and the Paranormal

I do not think anyone really knows for sure when a CCTV security system was first used to investigate the paranormal, but my guess would be sometime in the late 1970s or early 1980s, when the VCR made it possible to record what the CCTV camera saw and the systems became more affordable. The real question was just how useful were these security systems for paranormal investigating? The answer was and is pretty darn useful, and for more than one reason.

The digital age has brought paranormal investigating out of the dark ages and into the realm of legitimate scientific data collection, and the CCTV DVR system is a major player in the data collection we do.

Remember, we are not collecting evidence, we are collecting data. We then have to review the data to see if we may have captured any potential evidence of the paranormal. This potential evidence does not become actual evidence until, at the very least, the rest of your team reviews it and everyone agrees it is paranormal in nature, and there is not some other natural explanation for it.

The CCTV DVR system has become an invaluable tool in the arsenal of equipment that paranormal investigators have at their disposal and here is why:

1. More Eyes on the Case: It adds additional investigators to the paranormal team through the number of cameras linked to the system. Each CCTV camera is one more set of eyes that can constantly monitor an area where it is set up. In some ways they are better than people, in that the eye of the camera does not get tired or blink, and the recording of the image is not influenced by any potential prejudice of what it wants to see; it only sees what is there, be it an empty room, dust, or something unexplainable.

2. Unique Vision: CCTV IR cameras not only see in the dark, but they can see in a spectrum of light (infrared) that humans cannot. This is a huge advantage, as the recording then allows us to see in that spectrum through the eye of the camera and see what it sees.

3. Tireless: The system can keep investigating long after investigators have gone to bed; it does not get tired and can continue recording for days in some cases. The only drawback to this is that someone then has to review all of the footage at some point.

4. It Sees All: You can use the system to monitor the locations of your investigators by leaving one person to watch the television monitor at base camp. This way, with a small team someone can investigate a room that is being monitored without actually being alone, and if each team member has a walkie-talkie with them, then you have direct contact with that person. This also helps during the investigation and during data review for debunking what one investigator may have thought was something paranormal, such as a knock response to their question, when it was actually another investigator in another room bumping into something in the dark at the exact same moment. (Trust me, stuff like that happens more often than you might think during investigations.) It also helps to determine if something was in fact paranormal in nature.

These are some of the main reasons for your team to own and use a CCTV DVR system, but there are some other things to be aware of when using them. I would not call these drawbacks or disadvantages, but these are things you need to be aware of when using these systems:

1. Saving Video: Although most of these systems have a large capacity (500 GB hard drive or larger), if you keep footage from older investigations on the system's hard drive for too long, when drive space gets low some of these systems will automatically overwrite existing footage and it will be lost for good. The key is to review your footage before your next investigation and then download any segments that have potential paranormal activity. You can easily do this through the CCTV DVR system and save either to a flash drive or directly to a computer, depending on the options available on the system you purchased. They all come with directions on how to do this.

2. Recording: If this is the first time you have owned one of these systems, make sure once you have everything set up, that the monitor is on, and that you can view the cameras that are recording; otherwise you are going to get back from your investigation and wonder why you do not have any footage to review. On most systems there will be a red light that shows up on each camera screen indicating that

the camera is recording and operational. If you do not see that red dot or red light, then most likely the camera is not on and recording, which means you will have to go into the menu settings and turn them on to record. Remember, even if the camera is not recording to the DVR, you can still see an image on the monitor as long as the cameras are plugged into the system and they have power.

3. Video Quality Based on Number of Cameras: CCTV DVR systems have one small drawback from other cameras: the more cameras you run on a system the lower picture quality you will get, because the system has limitations in storage and recording quality. This is also why these systems come with multiple camera options, such as four-, eight-, and twelve-camera systems. Although a camera may be able to record at super fine quality, which would mean a huge file size on the hard drive, when you hook up all four cameras on a four-camera system, the video recording quality will be cut down to good to maintain hard drive storage space, meaning the image will be a bit pixilated/fuzzy, and will also be missing some information, because the video is now at sixteen frames per second instead of thirty-two frames per second. With a four-camera system you can record at the highest quality with only two cameras connected; with an eight-camera system you can record at the highest quality with four cameras connected, and so on. My suggestion for a group that is serious about investigating is to invest in an eight-camera system and run four cameras at the highest quality or six cameras at a slightly lower quality (twenty-four frames per second) if you need the extra camera coverage.

DVR System Setup

Let us take a moment to discuss setting up these systems to optimize your investigation, as well as what else you may need to make setup easy, optimize video surveillance, and protect your investment. Because the cameras these systems come with do not have anything to mount them on, you will want to pick up a few tripods. You do not need to go for heavy or expensive tripods, as CCTV cameras are pretty light. For my own team's system, I picked up four very inexpensive Vivitar® tripods. I like these tripods because they collapse to a small, easy-to-pack size which fit into the case I use to store the system, but they open up to a nice forty-one-inch height. The telescoping legs also allow me to set them up at different heights depending on the situation, or to keep the legs collapsed for simple mounting on a table or dresser. I have had these tripods for years, they are still going strong, and were well worth the investment.

Invest in a good storage case to keep your system stored and protected. You do not need to spend an arm and a leg, but get a good, hard case for camera equipment. I use and recommend the Zeikos ZE-HC52 Large Rolling Hard Case. It is relatively inexpensive and more than large enough to hold an eight-camera CCTV DVR system and your tripods, plus it is on wheels for easy mobility and comes with a large shoulder strap.

You will also need a television monitor for your system so you can set up and watch the cameras during your investigations. I would not go high-priced or too big; you only need to monitor the cameras. Keep it as simple and as inexpensive as you can. This television monitor should be dedicated to your CCTV DVR system and not used for regular daily home use. I prefer a seventeen- to twenty-two-inch flat screen monitor for these systems, as they pack away easily. Nineteen inch monitors are also very popular. When reviewing your DVR footage, you should review it one camera at a time, so a nineteen-inch monitor is more than large enough. You will want to protect the monitor, so you should also get a good storage case.

The best way I can explain setting up your CCTV DVR system on an investigation is through a few diagrams and these simple things to remember when trying to decide where to set up cameras:

1. Location, Location, Location: It is important to identify where paranormal activity has been consistently reported in the location you are investigating and set up your cameras in those locations. If you set up cameras where activity is reported on a somewhat regular basis you will increase your chances of capturing something paranormal on video. If you want to catch fish, then fish in a place where they are always seen feeding or have been caught before.

2. Stay within the Limits: All technology has its limits and CCTV cameras are no different: they can only see so far in the dark. Most CCTV cameras can only see from fifteen to thirty feet in IR night

mode, depending on the number of IR lights that are built into the camera. Know your equipment limitations and do not try to go beyond them, or you will just end up with poor quality video. If you are trying to cover a thirty-foot or longer hallway, set up one camera at one end shooting at a slight angle to see halfway down with the light illuminating a wall or a doorway, then set up another camera at the opposite end of the hallway and on the opposite wall, also at a slight angle to see the other way (see Diagram 1). This will give you good coverage of the hallway without trying to overextend the limits of the cameras.

This same concept applies to rooms, although small rooms will only require one camera, and you can get the best coverage by setting the camera up in one corner of the room as high off the floor as possible (see Diagram 2).

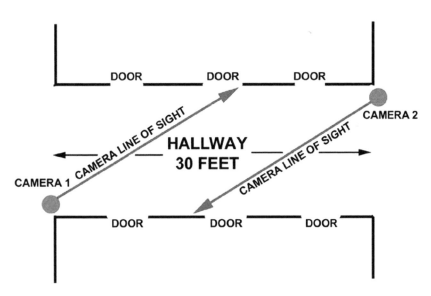

Diagram 1 – Recommended setup of DVR and/or mini-DV cameras to obtain best coverage of long hallways or large areas.

3. Do Not Cross the Streams: I know it is an old joke, but it really does apply when referring to IR cameras. Although all we see when we look at the IR lights on these cameras are some glowing red lights, the cameras themselves see it as bright white light. If you point these

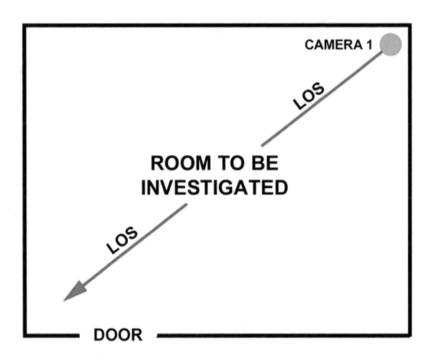

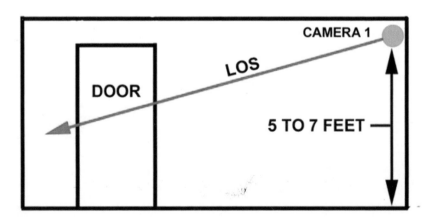

Diagram 2 – Recommended setup of DVR and/or mini-DV camera to obtain best coverage of a room.

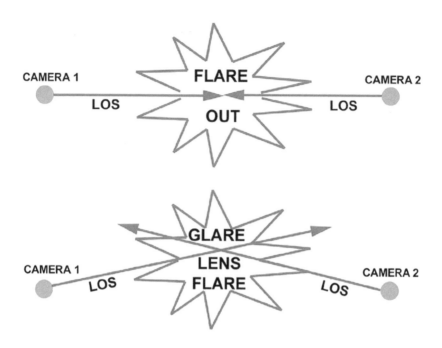

Diagram 3 – Since DVR cameras have their IR lights built into them, never face two or more of these cameras in the line of sight (LOS) of each other.

cameras at each other, all you will see is white light on your monitor, as the lights on the cameras blind each other's camera lens (this is known as flare out). This can also eventually damage the optics of the camera, because you are overloading the light sensors inside it. Crossing the line of sight (LOS) of these cameras (see Diagram 3) will cause glare and lens flare, making it impossible to distinguish what you are looking at during review. Is that something paranormal, or just one of the investigators walking in the background? I cannot tell with all of that glare in the camera.

E-Pods

These are fairly new to the field of paranormal research and investigation. Although popularized by some paranormal television shows, the actual advantages and usefulness of these devices to our field is still debatable; more research needs to be done with these devices. To determine if this item is something you want to add to your arsenal of equipment, I think it is important to

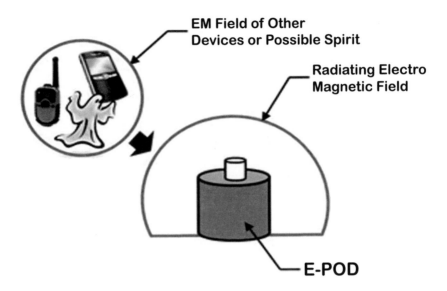

EM Field of Other Devices or Possible Spirit

Radiating Electro Magnetic Field

E-POD

Diagram 4

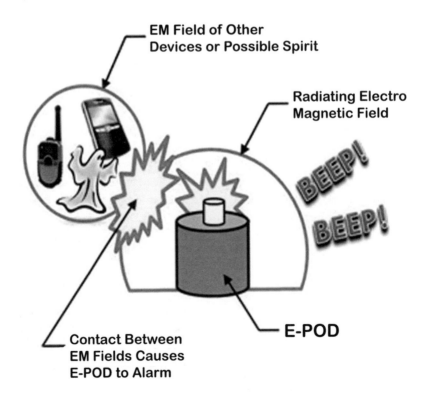

EM Field of Other Devices or Possible Spirit

Radiating Electro Magnetic Field

BEEP!
BEEP!

E-POD

Contact Between EM Fields Causes E-POD to Alarm

Diagram 5

understand exactly what E-Pods do; thankfully Pro-Measure spells this out in great detail on their website (http://www.pro-measure.com). Basically, the E-Pod detects high-voltage, electrically charged objects—objects charged with static electricity—at distances of two to eight feet, depending on the strength of the E-field being emitted. The E-Pod's detection sensitivity is as low as 500 mV (millivolts), making it a very sensitive device. To give you an idea of just how sensitive this device is, the outlets in your house are 110 volts (V), and it takes 1,000 mV to equal 1 V, so it takes 110,000 mV to equal 110 V. So how then is the E-Pod useful in paranormal research? If we accept the current theory that spirits are made up of electromagnetic energy, then they must emit some type of electrical field. The purpose of the E-Pod is to help the paranormal investigator detect the possible presence of a spirit through the electric field being emitted by it even at a distance, and thus help the investigator know when to try and communicate with a potential spirit, rather than the usual way of walking into a location in the dark and just trying to talk into the emptiness in hopes that there is a spirit there that might communicate. (See Diagrams 4 and 5 for a basic visual of how the E-Pod works and what can affect it.)

The real potential advantage of this device is for paranormal investigation teams who use a DVR system to monitor various areas when investigating a location. By setting up an E-Pod in each area being monitored, it would provide the investigating team with the ability to better monitor each location by having a visual and audio alarm in each room that is being monitored all night on the DVR system. Should one of the E-Pods in a room begin to light up—they also emit a sound as well, but it may or may not be heard by the team member monitoring the DVR—then the person monitoring the DVR system can notify the other team members of the activity and send them there to check it out if they desire. In some respects, the E-Pod is just an advanced KII unit, providing large, visual light output as well as a sound alarm to let you know when there is potentially a spirit or ghost within close proximity of the device that may be trying to communicate with you. It is much more sensitive than a KII unit, but at the same time, it is not an open device like the KII, in that the E-Pod is only affected by an E-field and not by cell phone signals, electrical appliances or equipment, or EMF emitted by home wiring. This device does have its potential uses and advantages for professional/serious investigative teams, but I really do not think it is worth the expense for the novice investigator or paranormal enthusiast.

The drawback of this device is that it is affected by electricity, especially static electricity. Even though you may set the E-Pod up in a location where you believe there is nothing to set the device off, just because it may suddenly light up and its audible alarm goes off does not mean that it was caused by a ghost. To understand why, we must understand the nature of electricity and how air can ionize due to weather changes, and even due to our own presence in a location. Although air is not the best conductor for electricity, electricity does travel through air, as anyone who has ever witnessed an electrical storm very well knows. Natural static electricity gathers in the air when positive and negative charges build up to a point where they eventually release the energy they create. Just because the E-Pod is only affected by electrical energy does not mean that when it activates it is a ghost causing it. It could just be the buildup of ionized particles and the release of that energy into the air.

So when using an E-Pod, how can we tell if we might be dealing with a spirit versus something caused by nature? Just like when using any other device to investigate the paranormal, repeatability is everything when trying to determine if you are possibly communicating with a spirit. An E-Pod is kind of like working with a KII: if you are in an area with it and you are asking questions, and you get multiple responses to your questions, you just might have made contact with an intelligent spirit. If the device lights up and alarms once or twice when you are asking questions, then it is more likely something non-paranormal is causing the device to react. As with any new device on the market for paranormal research, more field work needs to be done with it before the E-Pod's usefulness can be determined. For now, I would only suggest this device for serious paranormal investigators. If you are new to this field or just an enthusiast, I would recommend spending the extra money to purchase a higher end digital audio recorder or a Mel Meter.

Photography

As all paranormal investigators know, EVPs, disembodied voices, and unidentifiable sounds are the most common types of evidence we capture during investigations, but let us be honest: what we all truly hope for is to capture that one piece of visual evidence that will prove to others that spirits do exist, and that there is something more for us beyond this physical existence.

Since the first recorded observation by philosopher Mozi in fifth century BC China of an inverted image of a pagoda being observed through a pinhole, we humans have been fascinated with capturing images of everything and anything to share our interests and ideas, and express ourselves to others. The biggest door to photography was opened by Joseph Nicéphore Niépce in 1827, when he made the first photographic image using a camera obscura. Cameras have come a long way since 1827, but we are still using them for the same reason, to capture moments in time.

The Advent of Spirit Photography

What became known as spirit photography was first discovered by William H. Muller in the 1860s, when he found a second person in a photograph he took of himself and quickly discovered it was just a double exposure of himself. He soon found a way to make money with this by selling himself as a medium, taking photos of his clients and then doctoring the negatives to add in a client's deceased loved one and selling them the photos. As with all frauds, he was eventually discovered when he made the mistake of adding images of living Boston residents to photos as deceased loved ones.

There have been many more just like Mr. Muller over the centuries, and with advancements in technology and the advent of computers, Photoshop®, and ghost image apps, it has made it harder and harder to spot fake images, and even fake videos. It has gotten so bad that even long-time professionals in our field can be fooled now and then. The flip side is that the camera technology of today is giving us the best chance ever of capturing and recording actual paranormal and/or spirit activity. There are also some drawbacks to digital technology that we need to be aware of and keep in mind. Let us talk about the pros and cons for a few minutes before I get into the equipment that is available.

The Pros and Cons of Digital Camera Technology

The Pros: The digital age of photography has come a long way in a short time. Not many years ago, you had to have a camera to take photos and a camcorder to take video. Now there are cameras and camcorders that do both, and can be switched from one mode to the other with the simple click of a button or a tap on a touch screen. The greatest feature about these new digital cameras is the fact that you can review your photos or videos instantly. No waiting for film to be developed, no more lugging around a ten- to fifteen-pound VHS camcorder and VHS tapes. Now you have a combined camera/camcorder that can take hundreds or even thousands of photos and hours of high-definition video and store it all on its built in hard drive and/or microSD card. Cell phones can even do the same thing. Granted, the cell phone quality is not the best compared to cameras that are designed just for photography/video, but they can work in a pinch. The digital cameras of our modern age are the greatest thing that has come along for the paranormal community regarding investigation equipment in a long time. Most of these cameras can take high quality pictures in low light, and some even have an infrared (IR) function; and if they do not, they can be fairly easily converted to IR, ultraviolet (UV), or full spectrum (FS) at a reasonable cost. These spectrum options allow paranormal investigators to capture photographs and video in light spectrums that humans cannot see. They allow us to see what we normally could not see, and we have found that spirit energy typically can be seen in these far ends of the light spectrum. This, combined with the ability to instantly review the photo or video you just shot, opens the door to allowing the paranormal investigator to conduct real time investigations, rather than having to just ask questions, take random photos, and then go home to review everything and hope something was captured. The instant review allows the investigator to see if they captured any potential evidence while at the actual location, and to make on-the-spot decisions to move on or to stay in a vicinity based on what was or was not captured in photos or video. This increases the quality of an investigation and the chances of the investigator capturing real evidence of paranormal activity through the ability to make better decisions. Lastly, you can easily plug the camera into your computer to transfer images and upload them to the rest of your team over the internet for faster evidence review and easy incorporation into your reports.

The Cons: As with any technology, digital photography does have its issues and drawbacks, but it is getting better. Digital photography works much differently than film. In digital cameras, the images are not being transferred on to film through light exposure, so it is not a direct transfer of what you are photographing or video recording. Although digital camera technology works similar to a film camera at the front end—lenses, shutter, both in a sealed box to prevent incoming light—the back ends are much different. In a film camera, the incoming light is transferred on to a chemical film that creates an actual negative of the image it sees. The digital camera captures the incoming light on its light sensor array which transfers the light into computer binary code (ones and zeros) and stores that data on an internal memory card or hard drive. In other words, the internal sensor array and computer create a representation of the image the digital camera's lens viewed. Since the light data is interpreted by the digital camera, when the sensor array picks up light that it has a hard time interpreting, it will store the data to what it thinks best fits the light data the array is reading; this is the reason we see many more orbs in digital images than we do in film images. The sensor array is much more sensitive to light than film is so more light information is captured, but this does not mean that the orbs we see in digital photos are spirits; it just means the digital camera can see much more natural particles in the atmosphere than a film camera can.

Also sometimes the sensor array malfunctions, misses, or adds light data, and this can result in blank areas in a photo or video, or even the addition of something in an image that should not be there. When we see these things, we can sometimes be too quick to interpret these anomalies as a spirit or evidence of paranormal activity when all it may be is a malfunction of the sensor array or the wrong interpretation of the binary data by the camera. These are important things to remember when reviewing digital images.

The biggest drawback is the potential for losing your images and video. While the camera's storage can be pretty safe, it is usually during the transfer of your images and video to your computer where data is lost. One wrong click of the mouse and you can accidentally delete all your images, rather than transfer them to your computer. *Always copy* image and video files from your camera to your computer. This way, if something goes wrong during the copying process you will still have all of your original files safe on your digital camera's storage.

Digital Camera Choices

There are numerous choices and options of digital cameras and camcorders to choose from and all kinds of local and online shops to buy them from. Whether you are a seasoned paranormal investigator or new to the field, you still want to invest in a good quality camera, as you will have uses for it beyond your paranormal investigations. You do not have to spend a lot of money to get quality equipment. A good place to find digital cameras with an original factory installed IR option is on eBay.

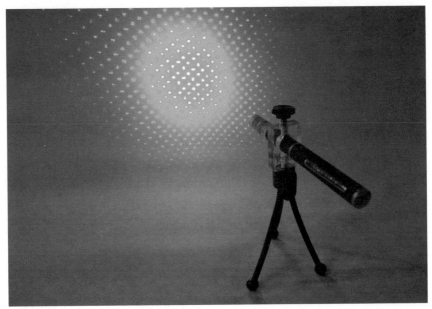

The truth is, many older model cameras are still high-tech and high quality for paranormal investigation. Many have been used once or twice at an event and were then put away, never to be used again. If you prefer your equipment brand new and a little bit more compact, then there are some other great choices you can find online or at your local store:

1. Canon VIXIA HF R42 2.07 MP, 32 GB HD Flash Memory Camcorder – Night and Low-Light Recording

2. Sony Handycam HDR-CX430V 8.9 MP, 32GB HD Flash Memory Camcorder – Night Recording

3. GoPro - Hero3+ – Low-Light Recording

All of these cameras will require some modification if you want to shoot in IR, UV, or full spectrum light. There are numerous sources online that can do these conversions for you. You can also purchase these cameras or similar models that have already been converted through online paranormal specialty shops, such as Ghostshop.com, Theghosthunterstore.com, and even Amazon.com.

Laser Grids

Although many investigators believe lasers are a new addition to the field of paranormal research, the truth is veterans of this field have been experimenting with the use of lasers to detect shadows since the first affordable laser pointers were introduced in the 1980s. These early, simple lasers produced a deep red light near the 670/650 nanometers (nm) wavelength. They were single beam laser lights and did not produce a grid like we now have available in some of the newer lasers that includes a diffuser (kaleidoscope) lens, which breaks up the single beam into multiple beams of various size and light strength, creating what we call a grid. Originally, lasers came in only one color (red), but are now available in red, green, yellow, and blue-violet. Each color is based on the wavelength in which it operates.

The most popular and widely used right now is the green laser. This also shows up excellently in the IR spectrum. The strength of the beam is measured in milliwatts (mW); the higher the milliwatts, the stronger the beam is and the farther the beam will reach. For instance, a 500 mW single light laser has an effective range—the range at which the light begins to diffuse—of approximately one mile when tested in a vacuum environment (i.e., space). It is important to understand that environmental factors have significant impact on the effective range of a single laser light. When the laser beam is diffused through a lens, the effective range of even a 500 mW laser reduces to about fifty feet or less, depending on the amount the laser light is diffused.

The original concept of using lasers for paranormal investigation was still the same in the 1980s: set up the laser and watch for something to break the beam. The lack of a grid in the '80s and '90s meant you could only cover a small region of an area you were investigating, such as the center of a hallway, or the threshold of a doorway, so its use was very limited, unless you were using more than one laser. This is why not much was heard about the use of lasers in paranormal research until the development of a micro diffuser lens attachment that allowed the laser's light to project a large grid pattern.

One of the first companies to release this lens with its lasers was LazerPoint® in the early 2000s, but the actual turning point for almost immediate and widespread use of the laser grid in paranormal research took place after it was used on the television shows *Ghost Hunters International* and then *Ghost Hunters* in 2010. Its use really gained momentum in the paranormal community after the airing of an episode of *Ghost Hunters* called "Haunted Hotel." During this episode their team investigated the Otesaga Resort Hotel in Cooperstown, New York. At one point during the investigation, two of the investigators went to the third floor and set up a laser grid. One of them explained that the purpose of the laser grid was to detect shadow movement using light patterns. After this episode that investigator was inundated on Twitter® and Facebook® with questions about the laser grid and where one could be obtained. The investigator posted on these sites that they had obtained the laser from a former member of *Ghost Hunters International.* I know this because I follow both of these people on these sites and read the postings, as did many others.

What most people do not realize is that some of these investigators involved with these shows used laser grids on numerous investigations outside of the shows, documenting their usefulness in capturing shadow figures and other movement. So this is the background of the laser grid and how its use in the paranormal field came to be, but is this device truly useful for our research? What benefit does it really offer to the paranormal investigator?

S.P.I.R.I.T.S. of New England, the paranormal team I am the technical specialist for, has been using the laser grid since we were first introduced to it by our friend Shannon in 2010. We have put it to use on every investigation since. In that time, I cannot say that we have captured any shadow figures with it, but that does not mean it has not been useful.

I have found that the laser grid is most useful when combined with an IR camera or DVR system for monitoring a room or hallway, but there is a limit to the size room these lasers can effectively cover. They are next to useless in a large, open warehouse, as the grid disperses too much and is not easily visible on an IR or full spectrum camera. I do not like to use them for anything over thirty feet, except for hallways, as the narrowness of a hallway keeps the grid confined and will allow for good coverage up to the point of the vision of the camera in these types of locations (see Diagram 6 and accompanying photo). When using them in rooms, I actually like to set up two lasers and have the grids cross each other to get solid coverage, especially in large rooms up to 30 ft. × 30 ft.; in cases like this it is ok, if not necessary, to "cross the streams" so to speak (see Diagram 7). In rooms smaller than twenty feet square you can use just one laser grid and still obtain good coverage of the room.

How does this help an investigation? The laser grid allows you to better monitor an area for any movement of any kind: not just shadows but also doors, door knobs, chairs, curtains—basically anything that is in the room/area you are monitoring. With the laser grid, if anything moves at all you are

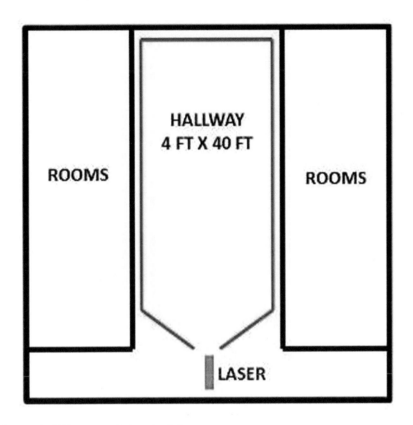

Diagram 6 – Grid coverage of a laser in a hallway.

going to know it due to a change in the laser grid. Also, if you are an investigator who likes orb activity, the grid can actually help you better discern between orbs, dust, and bugs, as dust and its directional pattern will be much more obvious in the grid, bugs will block out lights and cause distortion in the grid, and true orbs will actually not cause a distortion nor will they block out the grid lights; they will typically appear bright/glowing somewhat like the grid, but they will be moving through the grid, and because of the grid, you can better see when they first appear, their exact movement, and when/where they disappear, or move out of frame of the camera. So there is much more use to the laser grid than just trying to capture shadow movement/figures, and because of the low cost of these items, they are a great addition to any paranormal investigator's tool box. I would stay clear of the cheaper models and look for a laser with at least 200 mw output with a diffuser lens attachment.

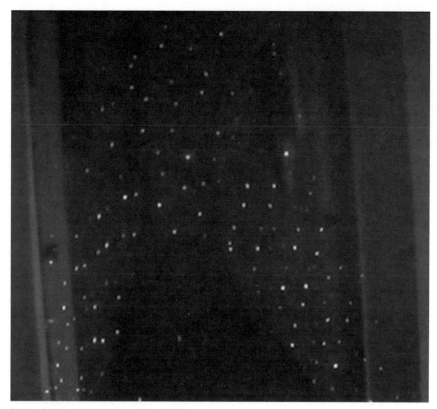

Photo of a laser grid covering a long hallway.

The only real drawback to a laser grid is its battery use. Most of these laser pointers use two triple-A batteries to power them, so you can expect to get about four hours of continuous use; be sure to carry extra batteries with you when conducting a long investigation.

Electromagnetic Pump

As paranormal investigators, we are always looking for the next piece of equipment that can help us make contact with the deceased, something that can be used to help make contact between us and spirits easier.

Given the fact that our primary theory, that the spirit—human, animal, or otherwise—exists as energy, and also needs energy to communicate and interact, then it would seem to make sense that a device that emanates electromagnetic (EM) energy would be a piece of equipment no paranormal investigator should be without.

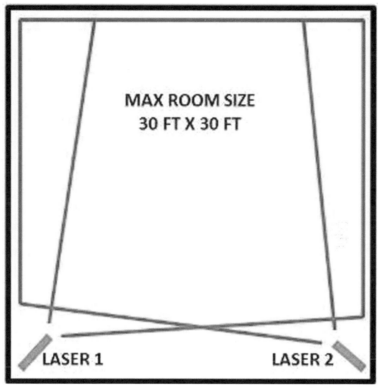

MAX ROOM SIZE
30 FT X 30 FT

LASER 1   LASER 2

Diagram 7 – Recommended setup for laser grids when covering a large room.

A device that actually emits EM energy to provide a spirit with a power source to draw from to communicate with us should result in outstanding investigations full of quality EVPs and/or direct communication through other devices, such as a KII, Mel Meter, or even an Ovilus. It would seem to make sense based on our theory of spirits and energy, right? The obvious answer would seem to be yes, but I personally have not found this to be the case regarding EM pumps, at least not yet.

I am sure at this point that some that have used EM pumps are disagreeing with my last statement. I am also sure some of you feel you have had great success using one or more of these devices, and maybe that is the case for you, but my own experiences with EM pumps and my own observations and analysis of their use have provided me with a different conclusion of their usefulness and actual impact on investigation results.

The EM pump is a device that produces and emits electromagnetic pulses which create a low-level electromagnetic field (EMF). This is somewhat different from the EMF that is produced by a building's wiring or fuse/breaker boxes, because those items radiate a constant, steady flow of energy compared to the pulses put out by an EM pump. According to the Digital Dowsing website—developer and manufacturer of the EM pump—once turned on, the device begins emitting a ".2 Hz pulse and increases to 256 Hz pulse." The EMF created by the pump is supposed to act as a beacon to any spirits that might be in the location you are investigating, providing them with a source of energy to use to communicate with. It is a sacrificial electrical source in that sense, taking the place of your camera, flashlight, or audio recorder batteries that can often be drained by a spirit during an investigation. This is the main theory behind the device.

The issue I have with EM pumps is that the field they discharge can also interfere with other devices we are trying to use to detect paranormal activity and attempt communication, such as electromagnetic field (EMF) meters, Mel Meters, and KII meters. Unlike electrical wiring, breaker boxes, and most appliances, the EM pump emanates a pulsing EM field, rather than a steady field. Although the pulse is at a regular interval, it makes it difficult to validate what might be actual spirit communication through one of the devices mentioned earlier or might just be interference from the EM pump. Although you can baseline the normal EMF of a room or location, once an EM pump is introduced into the environment, your EMF baseline is useless. I know some would say at this point that what I just covered is obvious and that the point is just do not use other EMF devices with the EM pump. That is true, and even the producers of the EM pump state it is best used for trying to increase chances of capturing EVPs and/or photographic evidence. They also state that the EM field emitted by the pump is very low—only four inches from the device—but it is best to keep your other electronic devices twelve inches or more away from the pump to prevent possible damage and/or interference.

Okay, so if the EM pump is not really useful with, and is perhaps possibly damaging to our other EMF devices, and the main use is to try and improve chances of capturing EVPs or photographic and/or video evidence, as it acts as a beacon to draw in spirits and provides them with a power source to draw from to manifest themselves and/or communicate with, then how useful and how successful is it at providing improved results for these specific applications?

I have done many investigations over the years, and on most of them I never had an EM pump. On my earliest investigations all I had was myself and a mini tape recorder. Even in those early days I was able to capture good EVPs during investigations where there was actually a spirit involved. So when the EM pump became available, I was of course interested in trying it out. I finally got my chance during an investigation with my friends from San Diego Ghost Hunters (sdGH).

We used one during an investigation of the famous Whaley House in Old Town San Diego. We set it up in the master bedroom on the second floor and let it run from one hour before we investigated that location until the end of the investigation. While we did experience a few things in that room and had some interesting words come through on the Ovilus, I did not capture any EVPs in that room or any photographic evidence. My best evidence that evening was actually captured in the front parlor downstairs, which is the farthest location in the house from where we had set up the EM pump. This was just one investigation. I have been involved with many other investigations since then where an EM pump was utilized to try and improve contact with a spirit, but I have seen no noticeable improvement in results when using this device. On all of these investigations, sometimes EVPs were captured and sometimes they were not, sometimes photo evidence was captured and sometimes it was not. There was no noticeable difference between investigations using an EM pump and those where one was not used.

What I have noticed is that some investigators have attempted to use their EMF detectors and KII meters in the locations they have set up the EM pump. They often get sporadic hits on these devices, sometimes while asking questions, and some of these investigators immediately believe that they are having direct interaction with a spirit, not taking into account the EM pump in the room and what it is doing. They tend to believe that the EM pump is the reason they are getting such increased spirit interaction because it is providing the energy the spirit needs to communicate. My own interpretation is that it is the device that is actually causing the EMF device to react due to the EMF the pump is outputting. Again, sometimes during these sessions EVPs are captured and sometimes they are not, so I see no real evidence that the EM pump is improving spirit communication or interaction, at least not yet.

While I have found that many paranormal teams and investigators use the EM pump, none I know of have actually conducted any serious comparison experimentation with this device. What needs to be done to determine the value of this item is to conduct multiple investigations in one known haunted location, both with and without the EM pump. To gather a good quality and quantity of data on this device, at least four investigations need to be conducted at a single location: two without use of the EM pump and two with the EM pump. I would also alternate these investigations to obtain the best data, and weather conditions and other environmental factors should be the same between each of the investigations, or at least between each of two investigations (e.g., investigations 1 and 2 should be under the same conditions, then 3 and 4). Also, the same room in the location should be used each time.

These are all control elements that will help validate the results of the experiment. For now, I can only suggest that if you own one of these devices, or if you are thinking about purchasing one, focus on exactly the type of evidence that the manufacturer recommends it for, which is EVPs and photo/video evidence. Do not use any type of EMF detector in the same room with the EM pump, as at this time I do believe it will only provide you with potential false positive hits on your KII, Mel Meter, or other EMF devices. You can also conduct your own experiments similarly to what I described above.

At this point I would not recommend an EM pump for the new investigator, new team, or the novice. The EM pump does produce a low-level constant pulsing electromagnetic field that can possibly be used as an energy source for spirits to draw from. Will a spirit actually be drawn to this source and will it use it to communicate with the living? It is possible, but here again, I do not believe there is any solid evidence at this point to support this.

The Ovilus

Mr. Bill Chappell, owner of Digital Dowsing®, has developed many unique devices for use by paranormal investigators; the Ovilus is probably the most unique and popular of them all.

There have been several versions of this device since Digital Dowsing first put it on the market in 2008. That very early version was called the Paranormal Puck, and it was eventually replaced by a more sophisticated version and was renamed the Ovilus. I will not get into each of the versions of this device, as many groups out there probably have the various versions, and now Digital Dowsing has released another new version which has some nice advanced features. What I want to focus on is the basic function of the Ovilus, which is to allow direct communication with spirits through its embedded word database.

Some versions of the Ovilus also contain several sensors, including an EMF meter, that take continuous readings of the surrounding environment. The device converts these readings into a number, and the number is then used to reference a word in the database. For example, if all of the environmental readings the device measures are converted by the device into the number ten, the device then looks up the number ten in the word database to see what word is associated with that number. If the word associated with the number ten in the database is *water*, the device will speak the word *water* (e.g., if environmental readings = ten and ten = water, then the device speaks the word *water*). Yes, it all comes down to a mathematical equation and a basic if/then statement.

The Ovilus can also be operated in its phonetic mode, which allows it to react to changes in EMF and to choose words from the embedded word database. In this instance, the Ovilus is converting EMF readings and calculating what the phonetic equivalent number is, then speaks a word based on its calculation. It all may sound more complicated than it is, but in the end, the real question is does it really work?

The simple answer is yes, of course it works. It does exactly what it is designed to do: gather information on various environmental changes and convert that data into a word and speak that word. Does the device allow spirits to communicate with the living? This is the real question and a bit more complicated to answer.

As someone once said, "To believe is to have faith, but evidence can make believing a lot easier." Okay, so maybe I am the one that said that, but you do need both in this field of work, especially when it comes to trusting the data/evidence that your equipment is providing you. So, does the Ovilus allow spirits to communicate with the living? Like all of the equipment I evaluate and report on, I have to base my conclusions on actual testing and use.

In the case of the Ovilus, based on my own use of it and my observations of other seasoned investigators' uses of it during investigations of known haunted locations with intelligent hauntings and of virgin locations purported to be haunted, I have come to the conclusion based on the data collected that yes, the Ovilus does allow spirits to communicate with us through the device.

I did not decide this lightly, and it took a lot of testing, data collection, and evidence review to come to this conclusion. I also came to the conclusion that although the device does allow for spirit communication, I do not feel that the communication that comes out of it is always accurate with what a spirit might be trying to convey to us. The device also has its flaws and bugs, as does any device, which I feel investigators sometimes mistake as spirit communication, but is nothing more than the device malfunctioning. So let me now get into the details of my use and testing of the Ovilus and how and why I have come to my conclusion.

My first time using the Ovilus was during an investigation with my good friends from San Diego Ghost Hunters® (sdGH). We were investigating the *Star of India*, which is berthed at the Maritime Museum in San Diego. My first impression of the Ovilus and the results it produced was one of interest, and also a bit of disbelief. At the time, I thought what was going on was that we were reading more into the words the device was spitting out than was really there. Although the responses seemed to be potential direct communication, I had my doubts.

The second and third investigations we used it on at the Whaley House and again on the *Star of India*, along with the capture of EVPs and other personal experiences that occurred at the same time we were getting responses on the Ovilus, began to change my opinion of this device. It was our use of it during a fourth investigation at the William Heath Davis House in San Diego that made me believe that the Ovilus does provide at least a good potential for spirit communication. As always, you have to keep a bit of skepticism when working in this field, especially with any device you are using, but what happened at the William Heath Davis House I could not just explain away, as it was completely unexpected, and the responses were accurate according to the individual who was with us and whom the responses/communication seemed to be directed at. Here is what happened there to make me less of a skeptic of this device and its potential as a spirit communication device.

We had been investigating the William Heath Davis House since about 9:00 p.m., and it was now about midnight. I had some very interesting personal experiences, including feeling dizzy every time I stepped into the doorway of the upstairs baby's room, but only in the doorway itself—if I stepped out of it or through it, I was fine. I also saw small green lights dart through that room from the adjoining bedroom, which had once been used as a hospital room for the sick when the building was used as a hospital. I also saw a dark shadow move through the bedroom. It was at around midnight when my friend and founder of the San Diego Ghost Hunters, Maritza, broke out her Ovilus to try and contact whatever spirits might be there. There were four of us in the room. I was the only male, and I sat on the floor next to the docent for the building who had joined us for the investigation. (I will call this woman Emma for the purposes of this book, as I do not want to disclose her real name.) Earlier in the evening I had heard Emma, Maritza, and Colleen talking about how Emma's son had recently passed. I was in another room at the time, so I did not hear much of the conversation, except that he had passed away recently. So there we all sat on the floor in the bedroom, with Emma to my left, Colleen to my right, and Maritza across from me. The ladies took turns holding the Ovilus and getting a few words here and there that did seem to have some possible connection to the house. Then Maritza and Colleen suggested that I try holding the Ovilus to see what interaction I might get. I took the device in both hands and tried to meditate as Maritza and Colleen directed me to do. I asked if there was anyone in the room with us and the Ovilus spoke the proper name, "John." Although this is my given name, everyone calls me Jack, so to be clear about what had just been spoken by the device I asked, "What did you say your name was?" Again the response was, "John." I looked at Maritza and Colleen and they both appeared excited and a bit shocked. When I looked over at Emma she seemed a bit distraught and stunned, but I had no idea why until Maritza spoke to her and asked her if she thought it could be her son.

The ladies could see that I was lost at this point, so they told me about how Emma's son, John, had just recently passed away due to an accident. Immediately after Maritza told me this the device spoke two more words: "Mother" and "accident." This startled me a little, but it also captured my interest in what might be happening. I asked another question, "John, is this your mother next to me?" Again a response came, "Mother." I asked, "Do you want to talk to your mother?" The response again was, "Mother." After this I continued to hold the device, but had Emma do the talking. What followed I have to admit struck me to my core.

Emma asked if it was indeed her son John and the device replied, "John." Emma asked if he was okay and the device responded, "Pain." I was informed at that point that he had suffered in pain before he died. If I was to allow myself to totally believe the potential conversation that followed over the next twenty minutes, then John was still staying by his mother because he was not in total acceptance of his death; he was worried about his mother, and he did not want to leave her alone. There was obviously a lot more detail to this interaction with the Ovilus than I have written here, but I think this is enough to explain my thoughts on this device and its potential for spirit communication.

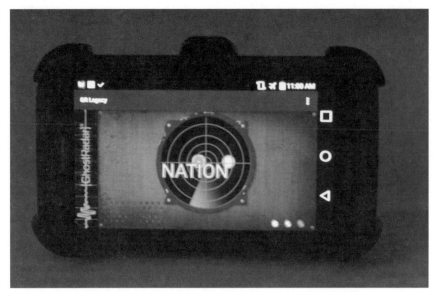

The thing that struck me the most about this potential communication we had was the fact that the communication was random. It had nothing to do with the house itself, as one might expect during an investigation, but was focused on an individual who was part of the investigating team. As the one who seemed to be the conduit between the spirit, Ovilus, and Emma, there was no possible way that I was causing the Ovilus to speak these words and responses, as until that night I had never even met Emma and knew nothing about her son, nor any details of his passing. This, along with the combined results of other investigations with this device, indicates to me that the Ovilus does have the potential to allow spirits to communicate through it. Is it one hundred percent accurate or effective? No. No device used in this field ever is.

No device we use in this field can detect or identify a ghost or spirit, or prove the existence of such. What the devices we use can do is provide us with data to review, evaluate, and draw our own conclusions. Based on the data I have collected and evaluated, the Ovilus is a device that can offer the potential for direct spirit communication. Is it the right piece of equipment to have in your arsenal of paranormal gear? In this particular case I would mostly recommend it for serious paranormal teams involved with trying to assist clients, or trying to further the paranormal field. I would not recommend it to the novice or weekend ghost hunter, as I do feel there are potential doors that might be opened with the use of this device, as it actually functions somewhat like a Ouija board. You hold the device while asking questions and wait for someone/something to respond, and those of us who have been in this field for a while know what can potentially happen when someone uses a Ouija board. On the lighter side, the other reason I do not recommend it to those just starting out is the Ovilus is a bit expensive. Is it worth the expense? It all depends on if you intend to use it or just let it sit in your box of paranormal tools and collect dust.

Ghost Radar® Application

There are very few paranormal investigators that do not own an Android® phone or iPhone® and carry it on them during an investigation. While we all know to turn them off, or to at least put them in airplane mode, or leave them back at base camp so they do not cause any interference with our Mel Meters, KIIs, and other EMF devices while investigating, there may be a good reason to take it with you as another investigation tool. Most of us in the paranormal field have at least heard of various types of ghost investigation apps that now exist for these phones, but how serious are these applications? Do they really work or are they all just fun and games? The truth is, most of them were just developed by programmers for fun, but the same thing can be said of the Ouija board or "talking board," which was created as a parlor game in the early 1890s, but as we all know became an early way to communicate with spirits and other non-human things that are best left alone.

After more than six years of research using an application called Ghost Radar®, I feel comfortable enough to say that yes, this phone application can be used to communicate with spirits and can be very useful during investigations to identify possible spirit activity and the presence of a spirit. Surprised? I do not blame you; I was surprised, to be honest. When I first decided to try out this app, I had major doubts about it, but I figured I would just try it for the heck of it; after all, the app was free at the time and I had nothing to lose using it. The first thing I did was read up on just how the app works and how it is supposed to be used. Here are the basics of what I found out.

1. The app uses a mathematical algorithm to analyze what the developer calls quantum fluctuations that are monitored through the phone or tablet. What the application monitors is changes in electrical energy within an area, then interprets those readings and

displays them on the screen as a red, yellow, or blue blip, depending on the strength of the energy fluctuation. This is meant to show the possible presence of a spirit.

2. The other part of the application allows for any potential spirit to speak through the phone or tablet and directly communicate with the investigator. This works similar to the Ovilus, in that the device will say words, and in the case of the app, it will also display and save the words spoken for the investigator to review later. I found this especially helpful when evaluating the usefulness of the app after investigations and comparing what words the application recorded compared to any EVPs that were captured at the same time.

3. It is important to allow the app to run for at least ten minutes after turning it on before using it to investigate. It often speaks words and shows energy fluctuations as soon as you turn it on, so it needs this ten-minute warm up period for the algorithm to stabilize to the surrounding environment. Ignore any information provided by the app within the ten-minute warm up period.

4. *Make sure your phone or tablet is in airplane mode* when using the application. Incoming and outgoing cell signals can interfere with the app and give false readings.

So how do I know this app actually allows a spirit to communicate with the investigator and can also at times show the presence of a spirit? I have been working with this app on investigations for the past three years and have collected and analyzed a lot of data over that time. The biggest surprise was the correlation between captured EVPs and words that were spoken by the app at the same time. Since it saves the words that are spoken, and also the time and date at which they are spoken, it makes it very easy to compare to EVPs captured on audio recorders, as well as the fact that the words that are spoken by the app can also be heard on the audio.

It is important to understand that the words spoken by the app rarely exactly match the EVP that is captured, but the word and the EVP are always synonyms. For instance, the app might say the word apple, but the EVP says fruit.

Sometimes you may also find the app will give you a response to a question you ask and the EVP you captured will confirm that answer, which would indicate you are dealing with an intelligent spirit. This occurred for me during one investigation at Fisher College in Boston. I asked for the spirit to tell me their name, and the proper name Alice came through the app, so I asked if Alice was their name and ended up capturing an EVP of a female voice responding, "Yes." This all occurred within the span of less than thirty seconds, and just prior to this the app had shown several energy blips on its screen, one of which seemed to appear right next to my fellow investigator, who said he felt something touch his shoulder. We were both seated at a table across from each other and he could not see the screen of my phone that was running the app, so he had no idea that an energy source had just appeared next to him just as he felt he was being touched.

I have documented many instances like this while using this app; far too many for them to just be coincidence or random. I have used this app on more than fifteen different investigations and have found it to be a very useful tool to add to the arsenal of paranormal equipment. Like any of the tools we use, it is not one hundred percent accurate and can be affected by other electronics, but when used properly, it can help identify potential paranormal activity and can help the investigator make contact with a potential spirit.

Like all the devices we use, we never know for sure if we are communicating with a spirit until after we review the data we collect and find the evidence that helps prove it. This app is no different—you still need to review all of your data after the investigation—but what it does do during an investigation is provide you with good on-the-spot data that can help you conduct a more thorough investigation and potentially have more meaningful communication with any potential spirit(s) that might be in the location you are investigating.

There are currently three iterations of Ghost Radar®:

1. Ghost Radar Classic (the original free version)

2. Ghost Radar Legacy (the second generation version)
- Has some advanced features for saving and e-mailing data reports to yourself or others.

3. Ghost Radar Connect (the third generation version)
- Has all the features of GRL, as well as the following advanced features:

- Audio recording button
- Image capture button
- Social sharing (Facebook®, Twitter®, etc.)
- Flashlight (LED) control
- Updated interface and graphics
- Improved detection

I have only worked with the Classic and Legacy versions of this app. Both work exactly the same, but I do like that the Legacy version allows me to e-mail the data report, which lets me print out the report for easier review during data analysis.

Thermal Imaging Cameras

Thermal imagers are probably the most desired tools by all serious paranormal investigators, and once again, it was the paranormal television shows that brought their popularity and potential usefulness to light, even though it was to the chagrin of the companies that manufactured them. The use of these devices for a fringe science like paranormal investigation was never a remote thought in the minds of the companies that developed them, and for a straightlaced engineering firm to suddenly see their device used on national television for reality shows about hunting ghosts is not what they considered good publicity at the time. Eventually they at least partially came around to this new use for their equipment, and the fact that their sales also increased kind of helped change their outlook.

Still, these devices are very expensive, and they are not very simple to understand and use correctly. Oh yes, they are easy to turn on and image with, but understanding what you are looking at, what the settings mean and do, and what settings to use under various environmental conditions is a whole other thing. Many investigators who are able to get their hands on one of these still have trouble grasping the fact that what they are looking at through these imagers is not video footage like with their IR cameras, but radiation in the infrared range of the electromagnetic spectrum.

These imagers do view in the IR spectrum, but not the IR light spectrum; they view the IR radiation spectrum, which is completely different.

In the years that followed the sinking disaster of the *Titanic* in 1912, numerous devices were attempted to be developed to detect icebergs; one of these was the IR iceberg detector patented by R. D. Parker in 1914. The next big development in IR technology came in 1929, when Hungarian physicist Kálmán Thanvi invented an IR night vision electronic television camera named the evaporograph for the British antiaircraft defense system. This device was so important to British air defense that it was not declassified until 1956. The biggest advancement in thermal imaging technology did not take place until after the release of the technical details of the device when Texas Instruments, Hughes Aircraft, and Honeywell developed single element detectors, which greatly reduced the size of the imager and improved image quality. Again, this technology was kept tightly guarded by the US military until it was finally declassified in 1992, and the technology patents were licensed by Honeywell to several manufacturers for production of these devices for industry and medical use.

Many more advances were made along the way to bring us to the compact, lightweight, handheld devices such as the FLIR® ONE Personal Thermal Imager.

A thermal imager sees infrared radiation in the electromagnetic spectrum; in simple terms, it sees the heat radiated by all objects—at least all objects that emit an electromagnetic radiation signature. By the way, EMF is the spatial expansion of the electromagnetic wave produced by electromagnetic radiation. This direct link between the radiation that the thermal imager sees and EMF is what makes this device a valuable tool for paranormal investigation; that is, if we in this field truly hold to our theory that spirits, at least intelligent spirits, are made of electromagnetic energy. This would answer the question of how the thermal imager is capable of capturing spirit energy, as well as the form it appears in. This would also then give credence to our seeming ability to communicate with intelligent spirits through various EMF devices and to detect their presence with them.

Does this device's potential significance to paranormal investigation mean it is a must-have for all serious paranormal investigators? No, it does not. It is a great tool to have in your arsenal if you can afford it, but it is not a necessity, not unless you are an investigator that is deep into the scientific end of this field. If you do happen to have a few thousand dollars to spare and want to purchase a thermal imager for your investigations, then you will want to know what to look for when buying one.

Unlike IR or full-spectrum cameras, picking out the right thermal imager is no simple task. Many of these imagers are designed for specific tasks, none of which is paranormal investigation. So how do you decide which is the right one to buy? Are any accessories needed? Who makes them? Where do you begin to look? First, if you are serious about buying one of these devices, do not go searching for one in online ghost shops; most do not carry them, and the few that do are typically selling used ones, which for the cost difference you may as well buy a new one direct from the manufacturer, or one of their authorized distributors, as you will get the advantage of a warrantee and their technical support team.

There are several companies that produce thermal imagers/cameras, but the top company is FLIR (http://www.flir.com). They are also the primary manufacturer of all thermal imager components. What this means is that no matter which company you buy from, there is a ninety-nine percent chance that their product contains FLIR components. This is not a bad thing, as their components are top-of-the-line. So now the search for a thermal imager comes down to what is needed for this line of work and the cost.

Honestly, I do not own a thermal imager and I am not likely to own one any time soon. But I have used them and I have had to do some research into them for my full-time job in the Department of Defense (I work as a senior engineering technician in weapons engineering for the DOD). Over the years some of the projects I have worked on required us to use thermal imagers/cameras to monitor various testing parameters we were doing, so it was my job to find one of these devices that would work for our needs. I contacted FLIR and other companies to see what was available and to have them do some demonstrations for us. Since that was a few years ago, I also did a little more research for this book into what is available today that will best suit paranormal research needs. The following are what I found to be the best options for paranormal work and the easiest to use. Both of these options allow video recording, and you can save the files as MPEG-4. The following are quoted right from FLIR's website:

1. FLIR T420 - Highest quality 307,200 pixel (640 × 480) resolution; 5 megapixel digital camera with LED lamp; 4.3" LCD touchscreen; 120° lens rotation; 8X digital zoom; Voice, text and

sketch annotation; P-i-P and fusion to superimpose thermal images; Bluetooth communication to MeterLink; WiFi connectivity; MPEG-4 non-radiometric IR video recording to SD card; Includes SD memory card, Li-ion rechargeable battery with adaptor/charger, two rechargeable batteries, 2-bay battery charger, USB mini-B cable, Bluetooth USB micro adapter, sunshield, stylus pen, headset, camera lens case, and hard transport case.

2. FLIR P-Series (P620, P640, and P660) - Powerful and interchangeable infrared lenses; 640 × 480 pixel resolution; High thermal sensitivity (40 mK [P620] to < 30 mK [P660] depending on model); All P-Series models include an integrated 3.2 megapixel visual camera, fixed lens, autofocus, and lamp for shooting in dark environments; The P-Series measures temperatures from -40°C to +500°C; Wireless remote control optional feature; Laser Locator; Easy access to composite video connection, USB, Firewire, and a direct connection to charge the battery inside the camera; Create visual and infrared non-radiometric MPEG-4 video files; Picture-in-Picture; Text and voice annotations; Automatic focus and manual focus, Digital zoom; 5.6 inch foldable high-quality LCD screen; Temperature sound, image alarms; and much more.

These FLIR devices do offer the best options and ease of use for what we as paranormal investigators need to do, without having to carry around extra devices to record video, or to easily download and review the video footage on our laptops, notebooks, or tablets. These represent the latest in compact cutting-edge thermal imaging technology. They are by no means inexpensive, but thermal technology is not as simple as IR or full-spectrum cameras.

The cost of thermal imagers is far less than it once was, but they are not yet in the price range that is truly affordable for the average consumer. For a serious paranormal team that wants to add another great tool to their arsenal of gear, the thermal imager can be worth the expense, and does become more affordable when the cost is divided among multiple team members, or if the team is officially incorporated, an LLC, or a non-profit organization, the expense can be tax-deductible.

Note: FLIR now has the FLIR ONE® Personal Thermal Imager. This device plugs into your iOS or Android phone (check the FLIR website for compatibility) and works with its own app and patented MSX technology to provide true thermal imaging at the most affordable price available.

Protecting and Organizing Your Equipment

A topic not often discussed with regards to paranormal equipment is how to keep it organized and protected between investigations. To most people this is a secondary thought over obtaining the equipment they need to conduct an investigation, but keeping your equipment organized and protected is just as important as having it. You can have all of the best paranormal investigation equipment in the world, but if you can't find it, or it does not work when you need it, then it is worthless.

I have been on many investigations with seasoned investigators and beginners, and it never ceases to amaze me how many people I see pull out a small duffle bag, unzip it, and begin to pull out their Mel Meters, digital recorders, EMF meters, IR camcorders, cameras, etc., all of it just tossed into the bag together, with no cushioning, no way to separate it, and no way to protect it. I even remember one person pulling out their snacks and drinks from the same bag, and after taking out their snack and drink just dropped the bag on the floor. I cringed as I saw this and heard loud clanking from all the equipment bouncing off each other as the bag hit the floor. All I could think was, "That's the end of those electronics." It turns out I was not wrong, as later that night, this same person was complaining to their friend that they could not get their camera to work.

I have seen things like this, and worse, more times than I care to remember. I hate to sound like a parent, but if you are not going to take care of your stuff do not bother wasting your money on it, because that is what you are doing, not to mention looking as unprofessional as you can get on an investigation when you show up with a duffel bag full of broken equipment and/or you are rummaging through it endlessly trying to find your camera, or the batteries you know you bought but just can't find buried in the pile of other stuff you have tossed into the bag. Things like searching for batteries or trying to fix damaged equipment also cost you valuable investigation time, not to mention money, as now you will either have to have the damaged equipment repaired or buy replacements.

The other thing that I see a lot of investigators use is the infamous "black vest." You know, the one with more pockets and compartments than a Marine going into combat could use. These vests can seem great, because they can hold just about every piece of equipment that you think of and all right at arm's length if you need it, but once you have this vest packed with your Mel Meters, camera, video camera, laser, batteries, etc., it will weigh you down and turn your ghost hunt into a cardio workout. These vests really do not provide much protection for your equipment, as even the top-of-the-line ones are not well padded nor waterproof, and the cheaper models are no better than the duffel bag. This is not to say that they do not have their uses or necessities, such as for investigators/cameramen on those reality ghost hunting shows who use them to carry their extra camera batteries, audio equipment, IR lights, etc., which they must have on hand during their investigations. They do also use the vests to carry some of their investigation equipment, but only during the investigation; they do not store their equipment in them. The investigators keep all of their equipment in foam-filled hard cases, most of which are water tight. But here again, these guys are not just paranormal investigators, they are also cameramen for the show, and for them vests like this are a necessity.

So what is the best way to organize and protect your valuable paranormal equipment without having to spend an arm and a leg on costly black Pelican® cases? There are a couple of great quality and affordable options for hard cases that will hold all of your equipment, keep it very organized for investigations, and well protected when not using it.

The first option at a reasonable cost are Zeikos® ZE-HC36 medium (18 × 13.5 × 6.5 in.) or ZE-HC52 large (22.875 × 14.125 × 7.5 in.) aluminum hard cases, as well as the Ape Case® Jumbo ACHC5600 (17.5 × 12.125 × 6 in.) or Ape Case® Extra Large ACHC5700 (22.875 × 14.375 × 7.25 in.) aluminum hard cases. While all of these are hard cases, I feel they offer the best equipment protection with customizable, diced foam interiors that allow you to fit your individual equipment perfectly into the case for optimal organization and cushion protection. I personally use the Zeikos® medium and large cases to store and organize all of my equipment. I have owned these for years now and have taken them on numerous investigations, and they are as sturdy and reliable as when I first bought them. When I open them up, I know and can easily see exactly where everything is and immediately grab whatever piece of equipment I need. If it needs a new battery, I also have three sections set up for those: one for nine volt, one for AA, and one for AAA batteries. Again, I know exactly where they are and can grab them quickly if necessary. I also do this for the special camera and IR light batteries.

I can fit everything I need for a small investigation into the one medium-sized case, which I can also take as a carry-on on a plane if necessary. For a large investigation I also bring along the large case, which holds four IR cameras, multiple IR lights, walkie-talkies, all the chargers/AC adapters for all of the equipment, a digital camera, light brackets, and even a couple of tri-pods, as well as all the necessary batteries, extra video lenses, and more.

I understand that not everyone likes hard cases, and for a number of reasons. Even a few of our S.P.I.R.I.T.S. team members do not like using hard cases because they feel they are too bulky, too heavy, and too hard to store in their homes. I understand these concerns, so I do have a few suggestions for soft cases that will provide a reasonable amount of organization, as well as protection.

The Ape Case Pro ACPRO1600 Case is a 20 × 12 × 8.5 in. soft case with sixteen heavily padded, configurable compartments, and also contains a padded compartment designed especially to hold up to a seventeen-inch notebook/laptop. If you have a lot of equipment, like what I carry in my large Zeikos case, then I would suggest the Ape Case Pro ACPRO4000 backpack with removable cart system. This is a well-padded and rugged case that can also carry a large laptop and is easy to travel with and store away.

Just because I mentioned specific cases in this article—some of which I use myself—does not mean I am recommending that you buy these specific brands. What I do strongly recommend you do is look for a good quality case—hard or soft—that offers high quality configurable padding or foam that you can easily modify to hold your specific equipment and accessories, and that will provide reasonable protection for your electronics from the elements. How much you want to or can afford is up to you, but I strongly recommend spending at least as much on a good quality case to organize and protect all of your equipment as you spent on the single most expensive piece of equipment you own.

The Human Factor

While this chapter has been all about the types of electronic equipment paranormal investigators use, there is one very important item I have decided to leave for last, as I believe it is the most important piece of equipment you take with you on every paranormal investigation: *you*! Without you every other piece of technical equipment is useless. What I am going to talk about here has nothing to do with using your technical equipment; it has to do with you connecting with and using your own human sensory system during an investigation.

I am not talking about trying to become psychic or meditating to connect with the other side. What I am talking about is recognizing what your human senses are and how to tune in to them when you are on an investigation to recognize subtle changes and odd happenings in your surroundings that might indicate something paranormal is either about to happen, is in the process of happening, or has just happened.

The five senses are sight, sound, touch, smell, and taste. But do we really know how to tune into each of them? Well at times we do, like during the holidays, when we smell our favorite meal being prepared and later taste its mouth-watering flavor, or on a hot summer day at the beach when we run into the water and feel its cool, refreshing sensation on our body, or when we touch or hold something new for the first time, like a newborn child, or when we are intimate with our lover and our senses are heightened and we feel, see, smell, and taste every nuance of our intimacy.

Most of the time we are not as in tune with our senses and we do notice things, but we are so busy with other things and other daily thoughts that we just tend to ignore what is not obvious—the subtle sights, sounds, smells, and changes that occur around us. This also happens to most paranormal investigators, even some of the seasoned ones. We can be so caught up in trying to get that EVP or capture something on camera that we do not notice what is or is not going on around us. The other side of the coin is that we may brush off that sudden headache, sick stomach feeling, or other physical reaction during an investigation as nothing more than due to fatigue, something we ate, or even an oncoming cold, when it actually may be our body reacting to the presence of something paranormal in nature.

So how can we tell the difference? What can we do during an investigation to help us identify when we are reacting to something potentially paranormal as compared to just something non-paranormal in nature? Let me tell you what I do, and what I recommend to every investigator who ever asks me about this.

1. Know Thyself: Do a good self-assessment before you go on an investigation. Know how you are feeling. How did you feel all day?

Are you tired? Do you have a cold? Are you hungry, not hungry? Are you feeling good? Did you get enough rest before your investigation? Are you feeling stressed, worried? Do you have any aches or pains, etc.? If your team is anything like the one I belong to, you will probably all meet at some place to eat before your investigation, after which you should do another quick self-assessment to make sure what you ate and drank has not had any serious effect on you. The point is that you basically need to take baseline readings of yourself and your senses just like you would take baseline EMF readings of a location you are about to investigate. You cannot identify changes if you do not know what you are starting with.

2. Get to Know Your Surroundings: To quote Bruce Lee, "Don't think, feel." When you do your walk-through of the location you are about to investigate, do not just think about where you are going to set up your cameras, recorders, and other equipment; take a moment in each area of the location to feel it. Use your senses to get to know that area. Is it hot, cold, or comfortable? Is the air light or heavy? Does it smell fragrant, musty, or somehow familiar? What color is the room? Is the lighting bright or dim, or is there any light at all? What is in the location and where are things located (furniture, appliances, is it empty)? If you are outside, what kind of night is it (overcast, clear, stormy, foggy)? What kind of shadows are being cast in the location? What noises, if any, do you hear? Again, it is important to get a baseline reading of the location you are investigating.

3. How Does It Make You Feel: I think this is the first question taught to every psychologist, but it is a good question and it can cover a lot; in our case, we want to assess ourselves on an emotional and physical level when investigating. For instance, when you enter a specific room or area of a location does your mood suddenly change? Do you maybe become nervous, anxious, afraid, feel ill, or do you feel like you just should not be there, like you are in danger? These can all be indications of a spirit presence, or that something out of the ordinary is taking place in that location. Suddenly becoming ill or getting a headache after spending only a short period of time in a location could also be a sign of something serious like a gas leak,

black mold, high EMF, or carbon monoxide fumes. All of these are health hazards, and if you find any of these during your investigation you should leave that area and report it to the owner. If you check and do not find any of these physical problems in the location, then it is likely something paranormal in nature is affecting you, and now is the time to start conducting that EVP session.

If you are feeling physically ill then just leave the location immediately and ask one of your fellow investigators to check out the location for you. Be sure to tell them what happened to you and exactly where. Also be sure another of your fellow investigators stays with you until you feel better. This is why it is important to work with a team of three or four investigators. I normally prefer four, but if there are only two of you then *stay together* and leave the area. Your safety is more important than any investigation.

4. Seeing Is Believing: We all know that as paranormal investigators, the majority of our work is done in the dark; sometimes it is not just in the literal sense, but also visual. What many of us do not think about when setting up all of the equipment when the lights are on is that once we shut those lights off it takes our eyes about twenty to thirty minutes to adjust to darkness, depending on the previous intensity of light exposure; this is a phenomenon called "dark adaptation."

Make sure you give your eyes time to adjust to the darkness before you try to begin your investigation. It is also safer, as once your eyes have adjusted you will be less likely to trip or bump into, or trip over something you did not see in the dark. Once your eyes have adjusted, remember that if you look at the view screen on your camera, then look back up at the dark, your eyes will need time to adjust again. This is also true when taking photos with a flash; anyone in the room will be affected by it unless they close their eyes first, so this is why we let others know when we are about to take a photo on an investigation.

Now that we are able to see in the dark, it is important to get a good visual of what is going on in the area; mostly we are taking note of the lighting and shadows in the area. Unless we are in the darkest of dungeons there is almost always some residual light from one source or another, even if it is our own flashlight. Take note of the shadows that are being cast by this residual light and the location of the source of the light; is it the moon outside, street lights, investigators' flashlights, the laser grid you have set up, etc.? Once you have a good handle on this keep watch for any subtle changes in the lighting. The best way to do this is to stay still and just watch to see if the lighting gets dimmer, or is blocked out altogether. Is there any movement in the shadows? Does your laser grid flicker or seem to suddenly change shape? Is something in the room suddenly blocked out by some dark mass? Can you suddenly see your own breath when you could not before? These can all be indicators that something paranormal is happening, but again, you need to know the baseline visual before you can notice any changes.

Lastly, if your eyes are adjusted to the dark and you see something odd then *do not ignore it*! Do not just brush it off as your imagination; tell your fellow investigator what you saw and check it out. In the work we do, it is better to assume you did see something than did not, as by immediately following up on it you may capture some good paranormal evidence, but by brushing it off as nothing you will likely miss out on a potential opportunity. Nothing ventured, nothing gained.

5. Can You Hear Me Now: Our hearing ability is an amazing thing, but it is also one of those things we tend to take for granted. Did you know that the human ear is capable of detecting pressure variations of less than one-billionth of an atmospheric pressure, and it can respond to minute pressure variations in the audible frequency range of 20 Hz–20 kHz?

What I have always found interesting and amusing is our human ability to tune into sounds that we enjoy, like our favorite song, and tune out those that bother us. We have all heard or coined the term selective hearing at one time or another. During an investigation, it is important to be able to tune in to the sounds of the environment around us, to try to pick out the usual from the unusual; is that just the building settling, or is that a response to a question you asked? Here again, the best way to be able to make these determinations is to get a baseline of your surroundings, and to do this you must first sit quietly and just listen. To help block out other distractions just sit down in the area you are investigating and close your eyes—this will also help with your visual adjustment to the dark. Do not move or talk to any other investigator you might be with and just soak in the sounds around you for several minutes. You will be surprised just how much more you will hear when you do this.

Once you have a good feel for the sounds in the area it will be much easier to pick out something that you did not hear before. Just like with every other sense, when you hear something that does not fit do not ignore it, ask a question and/or get up and go check it out. Do not miss that chance to capture or experience something that might be paranormal just because you thought it might be your imagination, just the building settling, or one of your investigators wandering around. Maybe it is one of those things, but you will not know for sure unless you check it out.

6. Be Patient and Stay in Tune: I have been on numerous investigations where me and another investigator were conducting an EVP session for more than thirty or forty minutes with nothing seeming to be happening, then suddenly one or both of us either got the chills, had a compelling urge to leave the area, or got a terrible headache. We stood our ground and captured some of the best EVPs we have ever gotten, and heard and captured a disembodied voice or saw a shadow figure. In one instance, we felt a significant drop in the room temperature, even though the room was already cold (40 F), and then captured an EVP and three shadow figures on our IR camera that were leaving the room we were in. In that case, for some reason I cannot explain, I just happened to pan my camera to the location the shadow figures appeared. I was not even looking through the viewer at the time, I just turned that direction and captured them on video. I can only chalk it up to the fact that I could sense something was changing in the room and I was in tune with it on a physical level, so my senses took over and I reacted to what I could not see.

A visual predecessor to this same incident also occurred just before the room got colder, as I was able to see my own breath for the first time that entire night, but it lasted for just a moment (three or four breaths). It is important to note that we were inside a closed and locked historical home at the time. These are the subtle little things that we as investigators need to tune ourselves into to help us be successful on our investigations.

During another investigation two of our people were conducting an EVP session when suddenly one of them felt sick to her stomach; it became so intense that she had to use the client's bathroom and did get physically ill. She passed it off at the time as just what she had for dinner, but upon later review of the audio at the time she began to feel ill, we found they had captured a Class A EVP of a female voice saying, "Dead in the swamp." In this particular case we obtained the assistance of a well-known psychic friend to help the client. Our friend told us that this female spirit had attempted to make direct contact with our investigator and that was why she became ill. What the spirit was trying to tell her was that she had been murdered in the swamp behind the client's home in the 1700s. Our research did validate that there was a settlement in that location in the mid- to late 1700s. We could not verify any deaths from that time period, but it is not out of the question that it could have happened.

7. Nothing to Fear but Fear Itself: I am going to step back a bit to address something I think is important when investigating the paranormal. I want to discuss the feelings of fear and anxiety that can sometimes come over us during an investigation, especially during times when we might find ourselves alone for a period of time, maybe because our fellow investigator had to go back to base camp to get something they forgot, to get new batteries, or even to use the restroom. Because the nature of what we do involves the search for spirits in dark and unfamiliar places, our anxiety is very likely already heightened, and when we are by ourselves in conditions like this our mind will begin to click into survival mode.

Our senses are automatically heightened and every sound we hear seems amplified, every shadow we see is moving, and the dark is foreboding and filled with danger. When we feel the hair on our arms and the backs of our necks stand up and we feel the room turn cold or the air become heavy, our gut tells us to turn and run . . . *do not*! Fear is a powerful emotion, but it can be overcome. Remember you are there to experience and capture evidence of the paranormal, and you cannot do that if you turn and run. The best way to combat this feeling of fear is to follow the guidance I have provided. Know yourself and get to know your surroundings before you begin your investigation. By doing this you are mentally preparing yourself for any paranormal encounter that might come along. All of this takes time to learn, and even those of us with years of experience are still learning.

You are the most important piece of paranormal investigation equipment you have. If you feel that you are one of those investigators who just never has anything happen during an investigation then try getting in tune with your senses on your next one. Before you just jump in asking questions to a potential spirit, sit quietly in the location for the first ten or fifteen minutes and get a feeling for the location. Try to notice any subtle changes to the atmosphere, any odd sounds or noises, any changes in the smell of the location, and any changes in how you feel or your own emotions. Then take time to introduce yourself and talk to any potential spirit, tell them why you are there, and why you want to talk to them before you jump in, asking them questions. Try these things and you just might find more is happening around you than you ever thought, and you might find that you start collecting more and better evidence of the paranormal.

Deane Winthrop House

Fairbanks House

Houghton Mansion

U.S.S. Constitution (Old Ironsides)

S.P.I.R.I.T.S.
Of New England
Supernatural
Paranormal
Investigations
Research
Intuitive
Truth
Society
SpiritsofNewEngland.org
Boston, MA
est. 2009

Paranormal
Investigations

Investigations by S.P.I.R.I.T.S. of New England

Even before our small group of paranormal enthusiasts founded S.P.I.R.I.T.S. of New England in January 2009, each of us had a deep interest in horror, science fiction, and all things strange that go bump in the night. When *Ghost Hunters* first aired in October 2004, it became a rallying cry for all of us now on the team, and many others with a passion for the paranormal, to search out other like-minded people that wanted to seriously discuss spirits, the afterlife, and all things paranormal.

The Atlantic Paranormal Society—otherwise known as TAPS—from which *Ghost Hunters* sprang had created what they called the Beyond Reality (BRE) online forum for fans of the show and the paranormal to gather, chat, discuss, and debate their passions for the paranormal. This forum is where we all first met. We would talk almost every night, sometimes for hours on end, and not just us, but many others, some of which are still good friends of ours, such as Frank and Sandy Follett, whose home in Connecticut we would later investigate with them, and who would later assist us from time to time on investigations.

These people touched our lives—some in good ways and some in bad—and helped us on our path to becoming the close family and strong seasoned paranormal team we are today. Our team has been through a lot together, and we have experienced and witnessed many things during our investigations that to this day we cannot explain. We have had a lot of fun, deep and meaningful talks, heated discussions, and we have even come close to breaking up at times, but in the end, we love each other and forgive each other, and that is what families do.

It is because of all these things that S.P.I.R.I.T.S. of New England is now able to share with you some of our investigations. These are the ones that have touched some or all of us on the team in ways we never would have dreamed. Because of this, at the end of each investigation one team member will share their personal thoughts about the investigation and the impact it had on them.

The chapters that follow are the detailed stories of just some of the investigations conducted by S.P.I.R.I.T.S. of New England; they are in chronological order, but the clients' names and addresses have been changed or omitted to protect their privacy. These are true stories about real people who have experienced and had their lives affected by actual paranormal events within their homes and places of work. Unlike what you see in the movies or on some of television shows, not all hauntings are demonic, but they can be negative, or have a very frightening and confusing impact on the people who experience them.

Helping a client to understand what is actually going on is ninety percent of the battle to helping put them at ease and be able to take back control of their home and their lives. Just being there for them to talk about what is going on is even more important to them than conducting the investigation. This is the heart and soul behind what S.P.I.R.I.T.S. is, does, and why we exist: to help people understand the paranormal regardless of whether they are a client, friend, coworker, or future investigator. We hope these investigations we are sharing will also provide you with a better understanding of what spirits/ghosts are and why they sometimes haunt the living. If nothing else, perhaps these investigations will just entertain you, but we hope they will teach you, or at least touch a part of your soul as they have touched ours.

CHAPTER 8
The Deane Winthrop House

The Deane Winthrop House at 40 Shirley Street in Winthrop, Massachusetts, is the oldest continuously occupied wooden-framed home in the United States. It was originally built about 1637, by Capt. William Pierce. In the early history of the American colonies, Pierce was one of the most celebrated and successful ship captains in New England. He was born in London prior to 1600, and is first noted in colony records as "Master of the Paragon" in 1622. Pierce was close friends with many of the early colonists, including Winthrop's second governor, John Winthrop.

Both the governor and Pierce were given adjoining land grants about 1637, and this is the property upon which Pierce built the original section of the house which is now the Deane Winthrop House. Pierce's home and properties were later acquired by Deane Winthrop, son of Governor John Winthrop, sometime after Capt. Pierce's death in 1641. The building was expanded by Deane Winthrop in the 1670s and is the same building that still stands.

The Winthrops were slave owners, which was not unusual in those early years of the colonies. The names of three slaves appear in Deane Winthrop's will of 1702—Marrear, Primas, and Robbin—all stated in the will to be of African descent. It is presumed that all three were laid to rest in what was then the "negro burying ground" at the northerly end of Winthrop Street (*King's Handbook of Boston Harbor*, third edition, 1888, pg. 133). The home was purchased by the Winthrop Improvement and Historical Association (WIHA) in 1907, and they continue to maintain the home to this day.

In August 2009, S.P.I.R.I.T.S. of New England was approved by the WIHA to conduct the first ever paranormal investigation of the house on their behalf. We would also conduct two follow-up investigations: one in December 2010 and one in April 2011. All of these investigations would yield solid evidence of paranormal activity occurring within the Deane Winthrop House, and would also lead to the likely conclusion that the home is still inhabited by its original owner, and perhaps even others who once served the Deane Winthrop family.

During S.P.I.R.I.T.S.' first investigation of the home in August 2009, we were limited in what we could do and how long we could investigate by the fact that we had to allow the ten members of the WIHA to investigate with us to gain access to the house. While this would normally make conducting an investigation very difficult due to the amount of people and possible contamination of the audio, the WIHA members were very respectful of our team and our rules that night, and also did a fantastic job of participating in the investigation.

We were able to capture some evidence that indicated possible paranormal activity in the house, which led to their request for the second investigation by our team. Prior to our first investigation in 2009, to obtain the background, history, and claims of activity of the house our team set up a meeting with WIHA's lead historian, Mr. David Hubbard, and also conducted internet research of the location prior to the meeting. We reviewed all of this information again before our second investigation and did some additional research on Capt. William Pierce, the Winthrop family, and details of the history of Winthrop, Massachusetts.

Background and Reported Activity

During our first meeting with Mr. Hubbard in 2009, he reported claims of odd cold spots appearing in the house, unusual voices being heard, and feelings of being watched in the basement and attic. He also told us the story of a young female child of one of the previous caretakers. The girl often told her parents stories of an old sea captain appearing in her room at night telling her stories about his voyages. The girl's room was part of the original house built by Capt. William Pierce and is believed to have been the captain's original bedroom. The girl is now a grown woman and does not remember any of this.

The last activity reported in the house was in August 2009, during our team's first investigation with members of WIHA. Our report to them revealed an interesting KII session in the attic with what possibly could have been Capt. William Pierce and another female entity. This KII interaction was witnessed by two S.P.I.R.I.T.S. team members and four WIHA members. We could find no EMF, intermittent EMF, or other electronic signals that could have caused this KII activity. Our team and WIHA members also experienced cold spots in the attic, bedrooms, and basement. We also experienced knocking noises upon request for them. We saw shadows moving in the basement and captured one Class A EVP there.

The second investigation in 2010 would be only the second time the WIHA ever allowed an investigation of the house, and the first time anyone was ever allowed to investigate it by themselves, although Mr. Hubbard would spend part of the evening with the team and would participate in part of the investigation.

The Investigation

The S.P.I.R.I.T.S. team, consisting of Ellen MacNeil, founder, case manager, and lead investigator; Beck Gann, founder and investigator; Sharon Koogler, cofounder and technical department lead; Sarah Campbell, investigator; Jack Kenna, technical specialist and assistant case manager; and guest investigator Eileen Kenna-Perfette, met with Mr. David Hubbard at 8:00 p.m., December 11, 2010, at the Deane Winthrop House. Beck, Sarah, and Eileen were given a tour of the house by Mr. Hubbard while Ellen, Sharon, and Jack began setting up equipment. Our team uses a four camera DVR system, seven Olympus digital audio recorders (one with each DVR camera and one with each team of investigators), two Sony mini-DV cameras, two Mel Meters with ambient temperature measurements, two electromagnetic field (EMF) detectors, and three KII meters on all of our investigations. We also use our own physical senses during each investigation to help identify changes in a room or location that our equipment may not detect.

Our team follows strict procedures and protocols to limit contamination, to ensure debunking is performed, to prevent any investigator from ever being alone, to ensure that no investigator ever acts unprofessionally in front of a client, and to ensure that as little time as possible is wasted on setup or teardown time. Most of our investigations last five to six hours, but sometimes longer.

Our second investigation of the Deane Winthrop House lasted six hours. We focused our efforts on the attic, the captain's bedroom, the basement, and what is referred to as the Historical Room, which contains many antiques and historical items from the 1600s through the 1900s. Some are original items from the home.

We set up our base camp in the kitchen, which is the most modernized area of the house, has the least amount of reported activity, and is the farthest location from the areas we would be investigating. We set up one IR camera in the historical room, one in the attic, and two in the basement—one on each side of the basement, with one looking east and one looking west to get the most coverage of the basement possible. We set up one mini-DV camera in what is believed to be Capt. William Pierce's bedroom. The other mini-DV was carried by Jack. One audio recorder was also set up in each location along with each camera to record throughout the investigation. An EMF sweep of the house was conducted prior to the start of the investigation. The average EMF reading was 2.5 mg. The highest reading was from the circuit breaker box in the basement, which read 96.0 mg.

The investigation began at approximately 9:00 p.m. Investigators Sharon and Beck went to the attic; Sarah and Eileen went to the basement. Jack and town historian Mr. David Hubbard went to the historical room, and Ellen remained at base camp, monitoring the DVR system. Considering David is not an investigator, our team decided to experiment with just focusing on a conversation about the home and the history of Winthrop with David in the historical room to see what activity might occur.

During the hour and a half spent in the room, the only incident that was experienced by both Jack and David was the sweet scent of what seemed to be pipe tobacco. Jack attempted to debunk this by checking for open windows or the smell coming from the street. Jack also checked for the smell coming from other rooms, including the basement directly below them. The scent was restricted to a very small area and moved from the back of the room to the front hallway, moving around objects and then completely dissipating.

Later in the evening, Beck, Sarah, and Eileen also experienced this same smell and could not determine its source. It again moved within the room, moved toward the front hallway, and dissipated. The first attic team of Beck and Sharon experienced a disembodied moan which was only heard by Beck, but was captured on a digital audio recorder. They also had direct responses on their KII unit to questions they were asking, including a yes response to a question by Sharon when she asked, "Was it you Captain that said 'hi' to Jack in the basement the last time we were here?" On our previous investigation in

The historical room where investigator Jack followed the smell of pipe tobacco through the room and to the stairway leading to the bedrooms.

August 2009, the only Class A EVP we captured was in the basement that said, "Hello Jack." Several EVPs were captured in the attic by three different teams, including "hey Jack" and the word "guns" after investigator Sarah asked if any of the guns downstairs belonged to Capt. Pierce.

A shadow figure was seen by Sharon in the captain's bedroom moving from right to left by the fireplace behind Jack. It was debunked as not being Jack's shadow, as Sharon had him move back and forth several times and walk around to see if he could cast the same shadow; he was not able to recreate the shadow that Sharon saw. Jack also had Sharon move back and forth from where she had been standing and it was not her shadow either.

EVPs were also captured in this room, and Jack experienced extreme chills and actual shaking of his body—like being sick with the flu—after asking whatever entity might be there to show him how to communicate with them; this lasted for about one to two minutes, until Jack asked whatever might be there to "back off please," then the feelings immediately stopped. A disembodied breath/moan was also heard in this room by the investigators. In the basement, Eileen and Sarah experienced cold spots, some of which were possibly debunked as being caused by a hole in the basement wall which led to the crawl space of the bathroom. Although some of the cold spots experienced were on the

The captain's bedroom where Sharon saw the shadow figure, where EVPs were captured, and where Jack experienced what some might consider a partial spirit possession.

opposite side of the basement from this hole and were localized—not a breeze—and would move, then stop, then disappear. Unusual flashes of bright light were also experienced, and were seen in areas where car headlights could not be causing them. The lights would have had to originate from the opposite side, where there were no windows, and beyond that wall would be the backyard (no road). The lights were small, bright, and circular, not like what is seen from reflecting car headlights. Several EVPs were also captured in the basement in response to questions and comments made by the investigators. One of those EVPs was of a child's voice responding "Right there" to one of the investigators asking where the cold was coming from.

Investigator Insights (Ellen MacNeil)

Having grown up in Winthrop, Massachusetts, just a few blocks down the street from the Deane Winthrop House, it has always been a huge curiosity for me due to its age (built in 1637) and its rich history. The house intrigued me so much that I eventually became a member of the Winthrop Improvement and Historical Association, which owns the house and property, and I became a member of the board of directors for the WIHA.

The basement where the EVP "Hello Jack" was captured, as well as the voice of a child. Footsteps were heard, strange light anomalies were seen, and cold spots were experienced.

The attic where KII communication with Capt. Pierce took place, numerous EVPs were captured, a disembodied voice was heard, and light anomalies were witnessed.

While I had spent a lot of time in the house over the years and heard many stories from other people and the caretakers about "unexplainable" experiences they had in the building, I had never experienced anything myself. After forming our paranormal team in 2009, I decided that the Deane Winthrop House was one place I wanted our team to investigate. When we finally did investigate, we and the WIHA were not disappointed with what we found and experienced. There was an EVP of a woman's voice saying "Hello Jack," to hearing a disembodied male voice in the attic saying "No" when one of our investigators asked Capt. Pierce if any of the guns in the downstairs historical room belonged to him, and numerous other personal experiences and evidence have been collected over the years. For us and the WIHA, the evidence we have collected validates that there are in fact spirits still dwelling within the home, and that Capt. William Pierce is at least one of those spirits.

The Findings

Based on the evidence we captured—the EVPs, experiences of the investigators, and the KII interaction captured on video—our team feels confident at this time stating that the Deane Winthrop House is active with paranormal activity and that the home seems to be haunted by the spirit of Capt. William Pierce— the original builder of the home—and perhaps the spirits of two other adults (one male and one female) and one child.

If you would like to find out more about the historic Deane Winthrop House, or wish to set up a tour of the house, you can find them on Facebook® at https://www.facebook.com/pages/Deane-Winthrop-House/108203052541421#.

S.P.I.R.I.T.S. of New England team founders (l to r) Ellen MacNeil and Beck Gann.

CHAPTER 9
The Houghton Mansion

The Houghton Mansion is a historic and famous haunted mansion at 172 Church Street in North Adams, Massachusetts. It was originally built in the 1890s by Albert Charles Houghton, president of the Arnold Print Works and first mayor of North Adams, for himself and his family. It was built in the Greek Neo-Classical Revival style. A North Adams 1876 map shows that prior to the Houghton Mansion there existed another home identified on the map as belonging to a W. M. Blackinton.

Further research revealed that this previous house was originally owned by a Mrs. Jane Cady, from whom William Blackinton purchased the home sometime around 1876. A. C. Houghton then purchased the house and property in the 1880s, and had the original house moved to another location

Portrait of Albert Charles Houghton hanging in what was once his office at the mansion.

in the city. This would be consistent with current local lore that the basement of a previous home was utilized and expanded for the Houghton Mansion. This local lore regarding the basement also ties to the supposed spirit of a little girl that haunts the mansion's basement. This little girl supposedly died in a fire in the previous home, but this story does not make much sense, as we know the previous home was purchased by Mr. Houghton, and we could find no records of a fire taking place at that home. I did find a death record for a Caroline Virginia Cady, age thirty-seven, daughter of Jane Cady of North Adams, Massachusetts, who died on 27 January 1876. Additional research revealed that this was the daughter of the same Jane Cady that owned the house at 172 Church Street in North Adams before she sold it to William Blackinton in 1876. So could it be the spirit of Caroline Cady, in child form, that actually haunts the basement of Houghton mansion? While it could be a possibility, it is unlikely.

Further research into the Houghton family did reveal another more plausible source for this child spirit. Albert and his wife Cordelia had five children together. Their first was a girl named Laura Cordelia, born on 30 September 1861 in Stamford, Bennington County, Vermont. Laura's death record states that she died in Stamford, Bennington County, Vermont, at age 3 years, 3 months, and 17 days. The cause of death is listed as brain fever. There is a slight discrepancy in the records on the date of death, as her death record lists it as being 13 January 1871, while her actual gravestone states she died on 17 January 1871. I believe this discrepancy has to do with the fact that while she did pass away in Stamford, Vermont, she was buried in Southview Cemetery in North Adams, Berkshire County, Massachusetts. This cemetery, and Laura's grave site, are on Church Street in North Adams, just south of the Houghton Mansion. Her mother Cordelia, father Albert, and sister Mary are also buried there. Mr. John Widders is also buried there, just behind and to the right of the Houghton family.

There are also some discrepancies in the records of when the Houghton family permanently moved from Stamford to North Adams. Information found states the family moved there permanently in 1870, but given the fact that Laura died in January 1871 in Stamford, it is more likely the family had bought a home in North Adams sometime in 1870, but did not make the final move there until after Laura's death in January 1871.

I always enjoy researching the history of a location, as it often reveals how over the years the facts of a story get distorted to better fit the legend created around an incident or a possible haunting, such as with the Houghton Mansion. It makes a much better ghost story that the basement is haunted by the spirit of a little girl that died in a terrible fire than if it might possibly be haunted by the spirit of a thirty-seven-year-old woman who died of natural causes but now seems to have come back in child form, or that the three-year-old daughter of the family who died of a fever is haunting the home.

The thought of a young life cut short in such a horrible manner as dying in a fire, and that you might run into her apparition in an old, dark basement, brings thoughts of all those scary Hollywood movies about demonic ghost children coming back to claim the lives of those they feel wronged them. The thought just sends shivers up your spine. Yes, it is a much better ghost story, but it is just not the truth. This does not distract from the fact that there are spirits residing in the Houghton Mansion, and given the true tragic story of the fatal car accident involving Mr. A. C. Houghton, his daughter Mary, her childhood friend, Sibyl (Cady) Hutton, and the Houghton's lifelong coachman-turned-chauffeur Mr. John Widders, it is no surprise that the Houghton mansion is truly haunted. Here again, if this ghost of a little girl is not that of Caroline Cady or little Laura Houghton, then who or what is it?

The Houghton family plot at Southview Cemetery in North Adams, Massachusetts.

Laura Cordelia Houghton, born September 30, 1867, died January 17, 1871. Her death record states she died on January 13, 1871, at age three years, three months, and seventeen days of "brain fever" in Stamford, Vermont.

The Accident

While I do not want to dwell on this event in the Houghton family history, it is important to discuss it to understand the likely reason for the haunting taking place in the mansion.

On August 1, 1914, A. C. Houghton, his daughter, Mary, her friend, Sibyl Hutton, and her husband, Dr. Robert Hutton, set out for a drive to nearby Bennington, Vermont, in Mr. Houghton's brand new 1914 Pierce Arrow touring car chauffeured by Mr. John Widders. It was a clear summer day when the group headed out on their drive.

At approximately 9:30 a.m., they entered Pownal, Vermont, driving up Oak Hill Road, when they encountered a horse team at a construction site on the road. Mr. Widders attempted to go around it on the left side of the road but lost control as the shoulder of the road gave out. The car rolled over the embankment, flipped over several times, and ended up in a field. There are various accounts of the accident and eyewitness accounts as well, all of which are well covered in the article "100th Anniversary, North Adams Mayor A.C. Houghton Dies Following Fatal Accident" (paulwmarino.org/fatal-accident.html). Still, the end results of the accident in these reports are all the same: Sybil Hutton died at the scene; her death certificate states she was, "crushed to death by an auto overturning." Her husband Dr. Hutton was thrown from the car but suffered no serious physical injuries. Mary Houghton was transported from the scene by another car to North Adams Regional Hospital, where she died. Her cause of death was listed as "accidental injuries to head, pelvis, and internal." Mr. Houghton was also thrown from the vehicle and suffered a fractured arm. Mr. Widders was thrown from the auto but suffered no physical injuries.

On August 2, 1914, Mr. John Widders, suffering from depression and likely shock over the deaths of Mary and Sybil, excused himself to a friend who was keeping a suicide watch on him. He supposedly went down to the horse stables around 4:00 a.m. for a smoke, as he had done on several occasions prior to this, but this time he was left to himself. His death certificate states he died of "suicidal pistol shot wound through head. Died instantly."

On August 11, 1914, Mr. Houghton died at home in his bed. While many stories state he died of a broken heart, the fact is he was very ill even before the accident, and it was Mary that took care of him. While we can be sure that he was heartbroken over the death of his youngest daughter, and this fact and the accident did have some influence on his health in those last days, the medical reasons for his death are listed as, "chronic inflammation of the heart, hardening artery walls and failing kidneys." All of which he was being treated for over the last seven years of his life. "Traumatic shock" from the accident was also listed as a contributing factor to his death.

Background and Reported Activity

Since it is well known and documented that the mansion is haunted, there are numerous claims of various types of activity over the decades based on personal experiences of individuals visiting the mansion and paranormal team investigations of it. Some of these claims are accurate and documented, but others, as with the history of the property and the mansion, may or may not be accurate, and may just be the product of overactive imaginations of people wanting desperately to experience the haunting of the building.

So how can we separate fact from fantasy when it comes to claims of spirit activity? In this case, because of the long history of paranormal activity, we can look to the reported claims for consistency, as well as look to the documented evidence of investigations of the mansion. The following are the claims of activity that we found to be credible and consistent:

- Hearing disembodied male, female, and female child's voices in the house.
- Hearing footsteps coming up the main stairway and servant's stairway to the second and third floors.
- Seeing an apparition staring out the third-floor window of Mr. John Widders' room.
- Seeing a light on in Mr. Widders' room, but there is no functioning light in that room.
- Seeing the apparition of a little girl in the basement.
- Hearing a little girl laughing.
- Hearing the side entrance door open and close when it is locked.
- Seeing shadow figures in the basement and on the third floor.
- Hearing the large doors to the Mason's temple open and close.
- Seeing the apparition of a young woman in Mary Houghton's second floor bedroom.

The third floor hallway to Mr. John Widders' room. The staircase is the servants' staircase, where disembodied footsteps are often heard.

The Investigation

S.P.I.R.I.T.S., along with guest investigators Michelle Kenna, Sandra and Frank Follett, and Mark, arrived at the Houghton Mansion for our private investigation on 15 November 2009, at approximately 7:00 p.m. We were greeted by our investigation escorts for the evening Nick and Breana, who were also part of a local paranormal group that managed the investigations for the local North Adams, Massachusetts, Masonic Lodge that now owns the mansion. Nick was also a member of the Masonic Lodge.

After a brief tour of the mansion, we set up base camp on the second floor in the office. This room is to the left after you come through the doorway off of the old servant's stairwell on the northeast side of the building. We set up our DVR system and then ran the cables to our four cameras. Two cameras were set up down in the basement in the long hallway that runs north and south. One infrared DVR camera was set up at each end of this hallway, so anything or anyone moving in the hallway, or just behind either camera, would be captured. This is also the same hallway where the apparition of the little

The Masonic temple at the mansion. Visitors and Masons have reported hearing the sounds of the temple doors opening and closing and the sounds of meetings being held.

girl is often reported being seen. There are also a couple doorways on either side of the hallway about halfway down.

The third DVR camera was set up in the second floor hallway near the main staircase on the south end of the building, where shadow figures were reported to be seen, and the last camera was set up on the third floor in Mr. Widders' room due to the activity reported in that room by visitors and Masons seeing the apparition of Mr. Widders and the non-working ceiling light being turned on. We also set up audio recorders with the cameras in each of these locations to be left running all evening, giving us the best chance of capturing any possible electronic voice phenomena (EVPs). I also set up one other digital voice recorder in Mary Houghton's bedroom, as I had felt a presence in that room and asked if she was there, to please speak with us that night.

Any other areas we investigated we would cover with handheld mini-DV cameras—which can also record in the infrared light spectrum—and we would each carry our own digital audio recorder to capture any potential EVPs.

Whenever our team is setting up our equipment, we try to be respectful of any spirits that might be in a location. We talk to them during our set up and tell them why we are there and what we are doing. We often even describe to them what the equipment is, how it works, and how they might be able to interact with it. Although I cannot really prove it, I do feel this is why we often get a great deal of activity on investigations. It is no different than talking to a live person; if you just take a little bit of time to talk with them and let them know what is going on you are more likely to peak that person's interest and they will be more likely to take an interest in what you are doing and want to be part of it.

After setup, our team split up into two groups of three, with our seventh member staying at base camp to watch the DVR monitor and keep an eye on everything and everyone. Ellen took the first watch at the monitor. Michelle, Mark, and I went to investigate Mr. Houghton's bedroom, as Michelle and I felt that room had a heaviness to it. Sharon, Sandy, and Frank went to the basement to investigate. Nick and Breana sat in Mary Houghton's room to allow us to do some investigating on our own without their presence. This also allowed them to do some investigating of their own in Mary's room.

After listening to the audio from that room in the days that followed, I was surprised and very pleased to hear Nick talking to the spirits of Mary, Mr. Houghton, and John Widders, asking them to please interact with us and telling them that we were good people and would be respectful of them. What pleased me most about this was that Nick thinks the same way our team does about the spirits, that they are/were people just like us, and that they deserve to be spoken to with respect and not be demanded to perform just so we can try to placate some egotistical desire to prove to others what great investigators we are by the evidence we capture.

I also know that Nick was not aware of the recorder in the room, so Nick truly understood what real paranormal investigation is about and that he had a deep respect for and even a connection to the spirits of the house, and he was passing that knowledge and insight on to Breana, a new member of their team. While all of this may seem irrelevant to the investigation, I would reiterate that I firmly believe this type of interaction with spirit is why our team, and others like us, have such success gathering evidence of paranormal activity.

Mr. Albert C. Houghton's room on the second floor where he passed away.

Mary Houghton's room on the second floor where many people believe Mary Houghton still spends time.

As our teams rotated through various locations within the mansion during the night, we all had some very unique experiences. What follows is a breakdown of the locations and what each team experienced there.

Mr. Houghton's Bedroom

Michelle, Mark, and I all experienced an extreme cold spot in one area in the center of the room. We also heard the laugh of a little girl. When I asked if it was Caroline and began talking about all of the children I have, I suddenly felt this cold spot on my lap while sitting in one of the chairs in the room. We also captured the EVP of an older male voice and a young girl in this room, and we had several knock responses to our questions, such as, "Is Mr. Houghton here with us?" and "Caroline, are you here with us?"

The Basement

Every paranormal investigator loves a spooky old basement, and the one in the Houghton Mansion is about as spooky as they get. The way the basement is divided into various rooms makes it almost maze-like and somewhat

The basement of the mansion, where the apparition of a little girl has been reported. Our S.P.I.R.I.T.S. team experienced and captured paranormal activity here.

disorienting, but that only added to the experiences we had down there. In the far back north room of the basement, even in the pitch black, we could see a small shadow figure pacing and darting back and forth in the far left corner. It seemed to be about the size of a four- or five-year-old child. Every team member saw this and each tried to debunk it, but could not. We also heard movement, like feet shuffling on the dirt floor, as well as what sounded like whispering voices.

In the long hallway area near the doorway to the furnace room my sister, Michelle, and I felt a coldness that seemed to be moving from one side of the hallway to the other. When I took out my KII meter and held it in the middle of the hallway it would flash almost up to red every time we felt the cold spot move. At one point I asked if it was Caroline, and could she please stay in one spot for a moment, and the cold spot stopped just in front of us. I was then able to get a constant spike on the KII meter and was able to follow an outline of this energy, which appeared to be about four feet tall by two feet wide—the size of a young child. This energy field then moved again and I was unable to find and track it. This energy anomaly lasted for approximately two minutes.

After this we decided to move to another section of the basement. We began to walk down the hallway, passing the heavy metal door to the furnace room on our right. As we approached the south end of the hallway and began to turn to our right toward the shop room we heard a loud screeching noise from behind us. We turned to look but saw nothing, until Michelle noticed that the door to the furnace room was now slightly open. We went back to it and I attempted to pull it shut. It was difficult, as the bottom of the door scraped along the basement floor. It was at this point we noticed the door scraping on the floor made the same sound we had heard, even more so when I opened it again. The question we were left with was just how did the door open on its own? Was it the spirit of Caroline that opened it?

John Widders' Room

While Michelle, Mark, and I were in the basement and Sandra was watching the monitors at base camp, Ellen, Sharon, Frank, Nick, and Breana were conducting an EVP session in John Widders' room on the third floor. During the initial tour all of us were in that room together, and we all heard knocks on the wall behind us while Nick was talking about Mr. Widders and the car accident that took the lives of Mary Houghton and her friend, Sibyl Hutton.

Mr. Widders' room, where our team experienced direct communication with the spirit of John Widders, and where team member Sharon Koogler was touched on the shoulder and hip.

The knocks seemed to get louder as Nick told the story, and then there was a large shuffling sound, as if something was moving within the wall. I looked back and noticed there was a small access door in the wall. I bent down and opened it, with Sharon right behind me to also try and look inside. I jumped back suddenly when an "arm" fell out from behind the access door! I nearly knocked Sharon over as I stumbled backward. As it turned out, it was only a dummy that the Masons dress up and use during their annual Halloween haunted house. I must admit it did scare me, but not enough to prevent me from climbing into the crawl space to see what might be making the knocking sounds.

Sharon and I could find nothing in the crawl space that would be making those noises: no pipes, no signs of mice, rats, or other rodents or animals, just boxes filled with various holiday supplies. We also noted that the knocks stopped as soon as we opened the crawl space door, so we even checked the door to see if it was loose or could somehow have caused the noise, but once it was closed it did not move. We could find no explanation for the knocking sounds we heard.

So during this third hour of the investigation, Ellen and the others were actually hoping to get Mr. Widders to give knock responses to their questions, but what they ended up experiencing was far more compelling and led to a unique experience for Sharon, who decided to spend the entire night in the room.

Besides their audio recorders, the group brought a KII meter in the room with them to see if they might get Mr. Widders, or whatever spirit might be there, to communicate through it. They began by asking if anyone was in the room with them and if it was Mr. John Widders. They asked for him to knock on the wall like he had during the tour, but there was no response. The KII was sitting on a chair in front of the window where the apparition of John Widders had been seen on several occasions. At first no one was really paying attention to it, until Sharon noticed it flashed after a question was asked by Ellen. She had asked about the car accident and if he was upset when people talked about it. Sharon repeated the question, adding that if it was Mr. Widders, he should make the KII light up once for yes and do nothing for no. The KII meter immediately lit up once for yes. This interaction with the KII meter continued for about forty minutes straight and took kind of a strange turn when Ellen asked John Widders if he liked Sharon, as he seemed to be responding mostly to her questions. The KII meter kept flashing as if excitedly saying yes. Then Sharon asked if he would like her to spend the night in his room and again, the KII lit up like crazy.

Nick and Breana began musing in amazement at the activity on the KII, telling the others that they had never seen anything like it before in the building with any other groups. The activity finally subsided and the group left the room, with Sharon promising Mr. Widders she would stay the night in his room.

At around 3:00 a.m., our team called it quits for the night. Ellen and Sharon stayed in the mansion for the night. Ellen slept in Mary Houghton's room and Sharon slept in Mr. Widders' room as she had promised. My sister Michelle and I stayed at a hotel in town. Frank, Sandra, and Mark all went home, as did Nick and Breana. The next morning Michelle, Ellen, Sharon, and I all had breakfast together at the mansion at the Mason's Sunday public breakfast. It was during breakfast that Sharon shared with us her personal experience while spending the night in Mr. Widders' room. The following is her personal account as she described it to me for this book, as well as her own insights about this investigation and the Houghton Mansion.

Sharon Koogler, cofounder and tech manager of S.P.I.R.I.T.S. of New England.

Investigator Insights (Sharon Koogler)

This is one my most favorite investigations for several reasons. It is a beautiful old house, and is almost maze-like inside. My most vivid memory of this investigation—and it is something that I will remember for the rest of my life—is sleeping that night in Mr. Widders' room and feeling cold spots—like hands—alternating between my shoulder and lower back. I was completely alone in the room, and on top of that, I was bundled in a sleeping bag, with no part of my body other than my head exposed.

My favorite bit of evidence from this investigation was the KII meter interaction in Mr. Widders' room. We had been getting some responses from a supposed spirit claiming to be John Widders, so I asked if he would mind if I slept in his room that night, using the usual "light up the device for yes" and "do nothing for no"; nothing lit up, indicating he did not mind. We asked more questions, then Ellen said, "So, let me get this right, you are okay with Sharon sleeping in here tonight?' The KII lit up off the charts. A while later Ellen said, "So, you are happy Sharon is going to be sleeping here tonight?" Again, the KII lit up like a Christmas tree. That was pretty amazing. We had

The headstone of Mr. John Widders, born October 18, 1880, died August 2, 1914. He is laid to rest not far from the Houghton family in their plot at Southview Cemetery in North Adams, Massachusetts.

been getting responses all night from him, but usually only a couple lights on the KII would flash; on those questions about me sleeping there it lit up completely. I still cannot fully explain what happened in the room that night.

Every investigation we do has a personal impact on us of some kind, but this one has left a lasting impression with me. I still wonder, was that a hand on my shoulder and back, or something else? It was definitely the most amazing experience I have ever had on an investigation thus far. It is something I will never forget and actually think about quite often. I sometimes wonder if John Widders would remember me if I went back, and to this day I would love to go back to follow up on that.

The Findings

Based on the evidence our team collected, the personal experiences we had, and given the long history of paranormal experiences by others who have visited the Houghton mansion, it is no real stretch to say that this location is haunted, or at least experiencing legitimate paranormal activity. Regarding drawing a conclusion as to what spirits may still inhabit the mansion, we can also safely say we believe the spirits of Mr. John Widders, Miss Mary Houghton, Mr. Albert Charles Houghton, and possibly little Laura Houghton still reside within the building.

At the time of publication, the Houghton Mansion has been sold by the North Adams Masonic Association to Houghton Mansion LLC and is currently no longer open for paranormal investigations. We can only hope that may change sometime in the near future, but in the meantime, it is good to know that this great historical location is being well looked after. If you would like to find out more about the historic Houghton Mansion in North Adams, Massachusetts, you can visit the following website: https://en.wikipedia.org/wiki/Houghton_Mansion.

CHAPTER 10
The Fairbanks House

It was the unique link between our team founder, Ms. Ellen MacNeil, and her participation in the Winthrop Improvement and Historical Society that led to the rare opportunity to investigate what might be considered the sister house to the historic Deane Winthrop House: the Fairbanks House in Dedham, Massachusetts.

These houses are the two oldest existing wooden homes in the United States. The Deane Winthrop House was originally built about 1637 by Capt. William Pierce and was then acquired by Deane Winthrop, the youngest son of John Winthrop, first governor of Massachusetts, in 1647. The Fairbanks House in Dedham, Massachusetts, was built between 1637 and 1641 for Jonathan and Grace Fairebanke and their six children. All of the precut timber for the original house was imported from England by Jonathan Fairebanke

Original items owned by the Fairbanks family displayed in their home in Dedham, Massachusetts.

and it still stands to this day. Over the years the house had additions put on as the family grew.

The Fairbanks House also has the very unique history of being owned by the same family since its construction first began in 1637. Today it is still owned and now operated as a museum by the Fairbanks Family in America, Inc. You can find out more about this unique and historic home at http://www.fairbankshouse.org/.

Our investigation of the Fairbanks House, per the permission of the Fairbanks Family in America, took place the evening of November 12, 2011. Our team was not the first to investigate the location; another paranormal team had conducted two previous investigations: one in fall 2010 and one in spring 2011. After quite a few conversations from June through October 2011 between S.P.I.R.I.T.S. team founder Ellen MacNeil and the Fairbanks House business operations manager at the time, Mrs. Lee Anne Hodson, we were cleared by the Fairbanks Family organization to conduct a third paranormal investigation of the house.

Background and Reported Activity

The long history of the Fairbanks House gives it great potential for possibly having paranormal activity, but there are many other factors and facts about the house and property that indicated to us that the activity and experiences reported by caretakers, docents, visitors, and Fairbanks family members might be more than just stories, or the work of active imaginations.

The actual personal artifacts of the family—shoes, hats, clothing, handmade quilts, handmade/painted buttons, dishes, tools, etc.—that were found and are still housed in the home make for the potential of strong attachments by a deceased family member to one or more of these items. A natural water source—a well—on the property just outside the main door of the house runs deep under the ground and under the house. The house is made completely of wood and timbers imported over 375 years ago from England, and wood, a well-known porous material, captures and retains scents, moisture, dust, and other residues from ages past through the present. Is it also possible that the wood and timbers of this home captured the emotions, activities, and perhaps life essence of the members of the family that lived there over the centuries? At least some of the experiences reported indicate that these factors do provide a catalyst for paranormal activity to be present. Here are a few of the experiences that were reported to our team by Mrs. Lee Anne Hodson and Mrs. Meaghan Siekman, the museum curator at the time of the investigation.

On numerous occasions over the years various docents, as well as Mrs. Hodson and Mrs. Siekman, have heard footsteps in the house when closing up for the night when no one else was there.

Mrs. Siekman saw the iron crane of the kitchen fireplace move when no one was near it and the house was being closed up for the evening.

When the house is closed up for the winter, or during the night when there are no visitors, various motion alarms and pressure sensor alarms in the floors of some of the rooms will activate. When investigated, there is no one found in the house and no signs of anyone having broken in or having somehow entered the home. These instances are investigated by the local police and the alarm company. No issues/problems are ever found with the alarm systems, either.

A young girl—a child of one visitor—reported seeing an old woman in the upstairs bedroom of the east wing during a tour. There were no older women

A view of the Fairbanks homestead from the corner of East Avenue and Eastern Avenue in Dedham, Massachusetts.

giving tours or on the tour of the house that day, and no one else on the tour saw this old woman except for the little girl.

Mrs. Hodson reported that in August 2011, she and one of the docents were working in the gift shop section of the house when they heard what sounded like someone moving boxes in the kitchen area. It frightened them so much that they ran from the house and stood outside in the pouring rain rather than stay in the house.

The Tour

Viewing the Fairbanks House for the first time brings to mind thoughts of a simpler time, a time before cars, paved roads, electricity, cell phones, and computers. This is a farm house from days long gone, when a living was earned by long days of hard work and one's own ingenuity. The amazingly good condition of this more than 375-year-old house speaks volumes to the hard work, pride, and love that this family put into their home and daily lives. Walking into the Fairbanks house is like stepping back in time. There are no frills or unnecessary architecture in this house. This is not a house owned by a family looking to impress others or trying to show off the wealth they had. This is a practical home, designed by practical people.

As you walk through the door you enter a small hallway; still, it is the wood structure that strikes you. It speaks to you of its age and stirs thoughts of those who have walked through that same door over the centuries. You are immediately faced with another old, smaller wooden door that leads up a narrow, steep, twisted staircase to the second floor of the original section of the house. To your right is what was the original living room with a fireplace, now used as the museum gift shop and the only room in the house with any electricity, consisting of one four-plug outlet (this would be our base camp where we would run the DVR system from).

To your left as you enter the house is the kitchen, one of the largest rooms in the house. The large brick fireplace with a cast iron swing out arm, large cooking pot, and small built-in brick oven to the left, and the large timber beams overhead with hanging skillets and other cooking tools, as well as an original antique flintlock rifle owned by Jonathan Fairebanke, tell the story of the family who lived there, the importance of family meals, and even how some of those meals were obtained through "God's" marketplace and the skills of the provider.

The other rooms of the house—the west bedroom, the lean-to section, the east living room and its former bedroom (now used as a display room for family artifacts), the east upstairs bedroom, and the two upstairs bedrooms of the original house—all silently speak of the family and its members who lived there, and how important family and the home was to them. Each room contains items and artifacts that once belonged to the family, and some contain items that were actually found within the walls and under the floorboards of the house.

On the property just outside the main door is the original functional stone water well. Births and deaths occurred within the walls of this house. It has also been witness to triumphs and tragedies. Walking through this house, one can sense its age and personality, and that perhaps, just perhaps, there is something intelligent about it, something still watching over it and the grounds upon which it has stood for over 375 years.

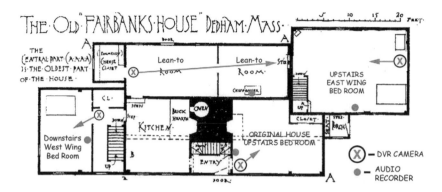

Diagram showing the locations of DVR cameras and audio recorders set up for our S.P.I.R.I.T.S. team investigation of the Fairbanks home.

The Investigation

For the investigation we set up four IR DVR cameras and four digital voice recorders covering various rooms of the house based on reported activity/ experiences (see diagram).

Several members of the Fairbanks Family organization joined us for the first two hours of the investigation, which began at approximately 8:30 p.m. We divided the members among our own team to maintain control of the investigation and ensure that our protocols were followed.

Our S.P.I.R.I.T.S. team that evening consisted of myself, Ellen MacNeil, Sarah Campbell, and Sharon Koogler. The Fairbanks members consisted of Meaghan Siekman, Katie and Justin Schlesiger—both Fairbanks family descendents—and Katie's friend, Fletcher. Justin, Katie, and Fletcher all serve as docents in the Fairbanks house during its open season, and Justin also sits on the board of directors of the Fairbanks Family organization.

We broke up into three groups: Ellen and I took Katie and Fletcher to investigate the upstairs east wing bedroom; Sharon and Sarah took Justin to investigate the downstairs west wing bedroom; and Meaghan offered to stay in the gift shop and keep an eye on the DVR monitor, so we instructed her on what to do and what to look for, and to write down in our notebook anything unusual she might spot on any of the cameras, even if it did not seem like anything significant to her.

By working the first two groups in these locations it put us at the farthest ends of the house from each other to help prevent any cross contamination.

The downstairs west wing bedroom where Sarah Campbell experienced the disembodied voice.

The upstairs east wing bedroom where a visitor to the house saw the apparition of an old woman. A light is sometimes seen in the window at night. This is where our team captured several EVPs of a woman's voice.

Sharon and her group investigated their location for a little over one hour, then returned to base camp in the gift shop. Justin left about this time, while Sharon, Sarah, and Meaghan remained at base camp. Ellen, Katie, Fletcher, and I worked the upstairs east wing bedroom for about two hours, as about one hour into our investigation we seemed to begin to get some possible interaction to our questions in the form of knock responses.

After two hours we then regrouped with the rest of the team back at the gift shop. We spent a short time discussing some of the things we had experienced, including Sarah hearing what she described as a very odd and loud noise in her ear while investigating the west wing bedroom which startled her so much that she dropped her flashlight. Neither Sharon nor Justin heard this noise, but it was captured on the audio recorder in the room. When played back during our data review, you can hear it is a deep male voice saying what sounds like, "Hello." In this same room Sharon also heard what she described as scratching sounds, and she saw a shadow move along the wall behind where Sarah was sitting near the bed.

After returning to the gift shop, and while the rest of us were still upstairs investigating the other bedroom, Sharon, Meaghan, and Sarah also heard what sounded like footsteps coming from what they thought to be the east wing parlor. They went to investigate but found nothing, and even called Ellen and me on the walkie-talkie to see if we had been walking around upstairs, which we had not. Ellen and I informed them that we had experienced what we believed to be knock responses to some of our questions and heard some other odd sounds that we could not account for, but we did not experience anything like what they had.

Upon review of the audio we had in that bedroom, I did find that we had captured two EVPs, both of which were very intriguing. In the first, you hear Ellen and Katie talking about a photo of some of the family members that had moved to the state of Maine at one time and in the EVP you can hear a woman's voice saying, "Show them Maine." What is significant about this EVP is that there is a large hand-drawn map in that room of the United States in the 1900s. The map was made by one of the family members at that time. Was this spirit trying to tell Katie to show us where Maine was on the map, or where in Maine they had moved to?

The second EVP captured seems to be in response to a question that I asked about whose bedroom it once was. The answer in the EVP is again a woman's voice saying, "The chil." Katie told us during our investigation of this room that it was once used as the bedroom for all of the children of the family. Is this what the spirit was attempting to tell us?

At about 11:00 p.m., we broke up into small teams again. By this time Katie and Fletcher had left, but Lee Anne Hodson had come back to check on us and asked if she could also investigate with us. Sarah and Sharon took Lee Anne and Meaghan with them to investigate the kitchen and lean-to areas while I sat at the DVR monitor with Ellen. This gave that group the chance to attempt to make contact with whatever spirits might be there without another group trying to do the same thing at the same time.

I always keep in the back of my mind that ghosts are people too—they just do not have bodies—and in doing so I do like to try and approach them as such. When two people try to carry on two conversations with one person at the same time that person begins to get confused, overwhelmed, and frustrated, and typically ends up just leaving both conversations. The same might happen to spirits when confronted by more than one investigative group trying to talk to them at the same time. By limiting the investigation to one active group, it might focus any potential spirit activity on the group and thus increase the chance of interaction. It is just a theory I have, but I do feel it tends to work more often than not.

The group spent the next hour investigating the kitchen and lean-to areas. Not much activity was experienced, but at one point Sarah, Sharon, and Meaghan all heard what they described as a dog whining, but they could not tell where the sound was coming from. One of the stories conveyed to us was that the last Fairbanks family member to live in the house had a pet dog that was somehow struck by lightning in the west wing bedroom and died under the bed there. This sound was also captured on the recorder in that room, as well as on Sharon's own recorder, and the recorder in the lean-to room. Upon initial review, it does almost sound like a dog whining, but after boosting the volume a bit and eliminating some of the background noise, it actually sounds like an old squeaky metal wheel of some kind being turned. What is interesting here is that in the lean-to room there are several old spinning wheels on display, all of which have not been used in many, many years, and have slightly rusted

The kitchen houses many original items of the Fairbanks family, including the rifle hung on the ceiling rafter. Both Lee Anne Hodson and Meaghan Siekman heard the sounds of items being moved in the kitchen when they were alone in the house.

metal spinning wheels. Did something move one of these spinning wheels, or was the sound they heard and captured on the audio recorders perhaps a residual sound from another lifetime within the house? A time when one of those spinning wheels was used to fabricate thread or yarn to make clothes, blankets, or quilts that the family needed.

A little after midnight, we all regrouped again in the gift shop and took a forty-minute break. We walked over to what is referred to as the bungalow, which is right next to the Fairbanks house on the property. It is actually the curator's house that was built by the Fairbanks Family organization in the early 1900s for the first curator, Mr. Henry Irving Fairbanks, whose spirit now supposedly still lingers in the building and still watches over the original Fairbanks house.

Because we were also told stories of Henry's activities within the bungalow, and because the evening was getting cold—it was 40°F outside and there is no heat in the Fairbanks house—Ellen and Sharon volunteered to investigate the bungalow's upstairs offices for the remainder of the evening, where most of the activity surrounding Henry Fairbanks was reported.

The lean-to area of the home, where the family made their own fabrics using spinning wheels and weaves. At one point during the investigation the team heard footsteps, as well as the sound of what could be a spinning wheel moving.

Sarah and I returned to the Fairbanks house with Meaghan to complete the investigation there. Even though Ellen and Sharon got the warmer end of the deal, I liked this idea because it allowed us for the first time to have almost no one in the original home while we investigated it. Meaghan was getting tired so she decided to just stay at the DVR system while Sarah and I investigated the last few locations in the house that had not been done yet. I actually would have liked to have the house with only me and Sarah in it, but because the house is a museum, by law and by the regulations of the Fairbanks Family organization, Meaghan had to at least be in the house with us as our escort, although she did not need to be in the same room with us. Sarah and I moved to the upstairs bedrooms of the original house to investigate while Meaghan remained in the gift shop.

The upstairs bedrooms are unique in their own right. The main bedroom is small and very, very crooked, with the floor sloping heavily forward and to the right toward what was the front (North facing) windows. The original sleeping area for the six children of Jonathan and Grace Fairebanke is actually the attic area above the main bedroom. There is a small wooden ladder that goes straight up the wall in the top floor landing to the attic, but it did not seem very sturdy, so we decided not to enter the attic section. To the right of the landing is the entrance to another bedroom that is part of the west wing addition and is directly above the west wing downstairs bedroom. We were told by Lee Anne not to enter this room, as several of the floor supports were removed at one time—no one seemed to know why—so this former bedroom is no longer considered safe for visitors to walk through, although several items, including a large wooden bed, are stored in the room. I decided to place an additional digital audio recorder on the floor entrance to that room along with

The old upstairs main bedroom of the original section of the home above the gift shop. This is where Jack had a sneezing fit and the EVP of a woman saying "Bless you" was captured.

my handheld IR video camera. Sarah and I then moved into the main bedroom to conduct our investigation.

This room is small (see image), but it also has a fireplace, a large bed, a small closet, a trunk, and an antique desk and chair. On the west wall is a small window, and there are two other small windows on the north wall. The room carried a somewhat musty, wooden smell, just like the rest of the house.

On the side of the east facing closet wall we noticed an old photograph that contained a lock of hair and what was possibly ribbon. The photo was of an older woman, but something seemed odd about it to me. I remembered seeing photos like this before and read about what they were. Then it came to me that this was a death photo we were looking at.

I have not seen many of these, but I have come across them from time to time at other museums and I have read about them. These types of photos were often taken during the 1800s. Because photography was new and very expensive, people did not have the money to spend to take family photos, but occasionally when a family member passed away, especially in the case of children and even infants, families would sometimes pay to have a final portrait taken of the deceased family member. This also made it much easier for the photographer to take the picture, as the subject was not going to move. Exposure times for glass plates to capture an image were much longer than with modern cameras, so a person sitting for a photo would have to stay still for a while; if the subject was deceased that was not a problem. So as time went on these types of photos became known as death photos as the subjects were in fact dead. Very often a lock of hair and/or piece of fabric, ribbon, or some other small item having belonged to the deceased person would be placed into the frame along with the photo for a remembrance/keepsake.

This was a death photo with a lock of that person's hair and other personal items. We began asking questions about the photo and the other items in the room, such as the hairbrush and hand mirror on the desk, and the bed. "Were these your items? Is that you in the photo? Does it bother you that this room is so crooked?" were just a few of the questions we asked.

We had not been in the room for more than ten minutes when I suddenly began having a sneezing fit. I say fit because it went on nonstop for over thirty minutes. I just could not stop sneezing. I did try to keep asking questions between sneezes and Sarah also continued to ask questions. Finally the sneezing stopped, and all I could think that might have caused it was either dust in the room or I was coming down with a cold, although I had no other symptoms that night, nor after we left that room.

After my sneezing finally subsided a bit—it never stopped completely until we left that room—we spent another ten minutes in the room with seemingly no activity. Here again, it is the data review that tells the true story of what may have been going on. During the first five minutes of my sneezing fit Sarah blessed me several times, but then gave up and focused as best she could on the investigation. All of this was captured on the audio recorder in the room and on the recorder in the other bedroom. There was also something else captured on the recorder: about fifteen minutes into my sneezing frenzy another somewhat whispery female voice is heard saying "Bless you" right after one of my very loud sneezes, followed by Sarah saying, "Too much dust up here," and then you can hear what seems to be a male voice saying, "Thanks," followed by another voice saying, "You're welcome," along with a knocking sound.

To me, these EVPs indicate two possible things. The first I believe is attached to something intelligent that was responding to my sneezing; the second seems to be something more residual in nature, perhaps triggered by my sneezing.

After finding these EVPs, I also believe that my sneezing may actually have been a physical reaction to whatever or whomever was in the room with us at the time. I believe this because of the fact that my sneezing began shortly after entering the room and stopped immediately after leaving the room, and these EVPs were captured in this room during our investigation, although we had no other experiences that would have indicated that we were in contact with a spirit, or had perhaps triggered some type of residual activity. From the upstairs bedroom we decided to head down to investigate the east wing parlor.

Of all the rooms in the house, the east wing parlor is my favorite room. This wing of the house was added sometime between 1780 and 1800—no one is exactly sure, as records on the house from this time are limited. What I love about this room is the corner fireplace, with its quaint mantel and triangular brick flooring in front. The room also contains the family piano, clock, artifacts, antiques, and portraits from various family members both famous and not so famous from throughout the centuries. It is the entire history of the Fairbanks family contained all in one room in a simple and organized manner, not cluttered or confused. This room speaks of the love this family has for their home, its history, and the history and honor of their family. Perhaps this is why the most compelling evidence we captured during our investigation was in this room.

Since there is also a small room just off the parlor, I decided to begin our investigation by sitting at the desk in that room while Sarah sat in the parlor. The idea behind this is that by allowing each of us to be somewhat alone in each room, even though we were only ten feet apart, it would be much less intimidating to any potential spirit that might be in the house with us, and would perhaps compel them to attempt to interact with one of us. This time I believe it may have worked.

The room I was sitting in was at one time the bedroom of Prudence Fairbanks (178?–1871), the eldest of three sisters that owned the house from 1843 to 1879. The other two sisters' names were Sally (1790–1877) and Nancy (1794–1879). The room is now used as a display area for some of the family furniture, personal items, antique dolls, portraits, etc. I was sitting at the desk, filming the room and asking questions, such as, "If you are here with us give us a sign, knock on the wall, show yourself." Sarah was working with my questioning and asking follow-up questions.

We had been in the location for about twenty minutes with seemingly no activity, and at this point I was getting pretty tired—it was now after 1:00 a.m.—so my tone began to go from one of questioning to that of provocation.

Chapter 10: The Fairbanks House

The east wing parlor, which also houses many original items from various generations of the Fairbanks family. This is the room where our team captured video of three shadow figures, heard footsteps, and captured EVPs.

The downstairs east wing bedroom where Jack first felt an extreme cold and could see his breath. It was shortly after this that he captured the video of the shadow figures in the parlor.

Still Image 1 from the video. Notice the light coming through the window.

Still Image 2 from the video. Notice the shadow figure that begins to appear in the room, blocking out the light in the window.

Still Image 3 from the video. The shadow figure is now more defined as it passes in front of the IR light of the camera and it completely blocks out the light in the window. To watch the video, go to our website http://www.spiritsofnewengland.org/evidence.html.

"I don't believe there's anyone here. Who would want to stay in this dirty old drafty house anyway." Then I decided to be more demanding, as if any spirit that might be there had insulted me, "If there is anyone here with me in this room you *have* to prove to me you are here. *Now*! No more messing around! We came here to talk with you at the request of your own family and you are being rude by not proving to us that you are even here!"

Two things are very important to take note of at this point: first, although it was cold outside and in the house, it was not so cold that at any time during the investigation could you see your breath or needed to wear gloves; second, the room I was in was extremely dark, so dark that the only way I could see more than one foot in front of me was through my handheld camera. Almost immediately after making my provoking demand for communication the room suddenly became much, much colder, to the point where I could see my breath even in the dark room. My hands became like ice, and I suddenly felt as though I was being watched. I asked Sarah if she thought it was getting colder where she was as well, and she said no, she was quite comfortable. I told her what was going on and she asked, "Are you in that room with Jack?" At that point the cold subsided a bit and I could no longer see my breath; it had lasted for only a few seconds. My hands were still like ice though, and my body was now freezing where before I had been comfortable, as I had continued to wear my jacket in the house all night.

I got up from the desk and walked back into the parlor to join Sarah. I had my video camera in my hands and was filming while walking around. I told Sarah I felt I was still being watched or followed by something or someone, and how cold the other room had gotten. She said she felt this room now getting colder since I came in and said she felt an extreme cold on her back.

It was at this point that my camera, which was now pointed in Sarah's direction near the fireplace and the south wall and windows of the east wing, captured something that to this day our team has not been able to debunk. This was something I did not see at the time, as I was not even looking through the view finder of the camera. I cannot even say for sure why I filmed in the location that I did, or why I moved the camera in the directions that I did, except that at the time I know that I felt there was something or someone in the room with us. What we later found during review was that the camera had captured three very distinct shadows moving past the window behind Sarah, all of which blocked out a street light that was shining through the window, and all of which moved behind Sarah from right to left (from the direction of the old bedroom toward the lean-to room), then disappeared into the shadows. Although they moved along the wall, they were not on the wall. They all seemed to be in front of the south wall and were in the room with us. Although it is not possible to show the video in this book, I have pulled three still images from the video that I hope will show you the progression of at least one of these shadow figures (see pgs. 144–145). Also, an EVP was captured on my audio recorder at the same time, although not on the audio of the video camera. On the audio recorder you can hear a voice saying, "Good night" just as the shadows are captured.

Investigator Insights (Sarah Campbell)

I have to give credit to the spirits in the Fairbanks house, as this was the first spirit that actually managed to give me a good scare. I was sitting down on the floor in the east wing bedroom with two other people in front of me, and then over my shoulder I heard an odd voice cry out, and I was the only one who heard it! It was clear as a bell; there was no mistaking it for something

Sarah Campbell, daughter of Ellen MacNeil and Beck Gann, and an investigator with S.P.I.R.I.T.S. of New England.

falling over or an animal crying out. There was a little path between the wall and the bed that I was leaning against, and the voice came from there. Like the brave investigator I am, I had a mini-heart attack and jumped half a foot, tossing my flashlight on to the floor and giving everyone else a little fright. Though the recorders did not catch the sound I heard, we were still able to hear someone attempting to communicate with us, and that is certainly power worth acknowledging. It is really an honor to think back and know that someone else was there and did actually want to speak with us.

Regarding the video evidence captured of the shadow figures moving across the room, I would like to say this: any sane person might have actually freaked out with the knowledge of three spirits walking past you while you sat clueless on the floor. My personal enjoyment of this piece of evidence comes in two parts. One, the evidence itself; how remarkable is it to catch multiple shadow figures moving on camera? That is, in my opinion, the pièce de résistance or Holy Grail of evidence. It is evidence like this that every paranormal team hopes to capture. It is such a rare occurrence, and yet we were fortunate enough to obtain it.

The second part comes from our second visit to the Fairbanks house and our attempt to debunk the shadow figures we caught. We went out of our way, spending over three hours to attempt to recreate these shadows, with no luck. Yet even without the answers we were looking for, the team proved its worth and did not become starry-eyed over a single clip of ghostly evidence. We wanted to prove or disprove this piece of potential evidence, refusing to show it to our clients before we were thoroughly satisfied—at least as much as one can be in this field—with our conclusions about it.

Credibility is everything in the field of paranormal research; even though you may think you have a great piece of evidence, you have to sometimes go to extreme lengths to try to disprove that potential piece of extraordinary evidence you just captured before you can feel at ease presenting it to your client as true evidence of paranormal activity. If you do not attempt to disprove it, then you do your client, yourself, and the rest of the paranormal field a great disservice, especially if it ends up being debunked by either your own client or another paranormal team once scrutinized. You have to do your homework, and you have to be willing to sometimes concede that what you thought was a great piece of evidence is either just a trick of the light or it has a more normal rather than paranormal explanation for it.

The Findings

The Fairbanks house in Dedham, Massachusetts, is a home that contains the historic wealth of a family that helped found and settle America. The heritage of this family is truly reflective of the heritage of the United States. Members of their family have served this country as farmers, pastors, doctors, scientists, Army officers, judges, and even as vice president of the United States under Teddy Roosevelt. Even the city of Fairbanks, Alaska, is named in honor of Vice President Charles Warren Fairbanks. With such great history and artifacts all housed within this modest Puritan family home, is it really any wonder that we should find that this location is still presided over by one or more of the spirits of its honorable, hardworking, and loving family members? So should you ever find yourself in the Boston, Massachusetts, area, I strongly recommend you take the opportunity to make the thirty-minute drive down Interstate I-93 to I-95 and East Street, and into the town of Dedham, and make a visit to this beautiful, dignified, and well cared for Puritan homestead where you can view the historic life of this unique American family and perhaps, just perhaps, experience the presence of Henry, Prudence, Sally, Nancy, or other possible family members that seem to still be keeping vigil over their beloved home.

CHAPTER 11

The USS *Constitution* (Old Iron Sides)

In April 2010, S.P.I.R.I.T.S. of New England founder Ellen Mac-Neil contacted the US Navy public relations office for the USS *Constitution* at the Charlestown Navy Yard in Charlestown, Massachusetts. She made a request for our team to be allowed to investigate the historical USS *Constitution*, also referred to as Old Iron Sides, the oldest commissioned Navy ship in the US Navy and the world.

The USS *Constitution* is a forty-four-gun frigate built in Boston, Massachusetts, and launched on October 27, 1797. It is the only remaining frigate of a total of six authorized under the Naval Armament Act signed into law by President George Washington on March 27, 1794. Although best known for her combat record during the War of 1812, the USS *Constitution* had built a strong reputation for herself during the Quasi-War with France (1798–1801) and the Barbary Wars (1801–1805), having won all of her engagements in both wars. The USS *Constitution* was taken out of active service in 1855, but she remains a commissioned ship of the US Navy to this day. She was given the unique title "America's Ship of State" by act of Congress in October 2009. During her long history, over three hundred of her crew died during service to this great ship and its country. Of all of those deaths, only a handful died during combat. The majority of the deaths were due to accidents, drownings, and most often disease.

Within one week of Ms. MacNeil's request, the S.P.I.R.I.T.S. of New England team was granted permission by then Commander (CDR) Timothy M. Cooper of the USS *Constitution* to conduct a paranormal investigation of the ship to attempt to obtain some answers for the ship's officers and crew, as many of them reported experiencing strange events on the ship. In recent months it had gotten to the point where some crew members were even afraid to work night duty on the ship due to the activity they were experiencing. The reports of odd occurrences had increased during her recent repair period that began in 2007, and was scheduled to be completed by November 2010. What crew members reported experiencing during the day, and especially at night, on the ship included:

1. Feelings of being watched/followed.

2. Hearing footsteps behind them or on the deck above them when no one else was on board.

3. Locked doors being found open.

4. Hearing voices near them (again, when they were alone on the ship).

5. Seeing shadow figures on the main gun deck.

6. The ship's American flag had been laid out on orlop deck to dry out after a rain storm and it was captured on the ship's security camera moving as if a breeze had gotten under it, but there are no port openings on that deck and no vents of any kind. They could not explain how the flag moved the way it did.

7. Finding small bare footprints on the top deck, as if a young person had stepped in water and walked across the deck, but the footprints would start in the center of the deck and there would only be four or five prints before they ended.

8. Seeing a young boy on the ship in the evening after the ship was closed to visitors. When crew would go to talk to the boy he would just be gone.

The S.P.I.R.I.T.S. team requested two nights to be able to conduct a thorough investigation of the ship. CDR Cooper agreed, and the investigation dates were set for June 25–27, 2010, from 7:00 p.m. to 3:00 a.m. each night. The team would also have an escort with them each night that would be one of the ship's officers.

25 June 2010, 5:00 P.M., Charlestown, Massachusetts

The S.P.I.R.I.T.S. team arrived at the Charlestown Navy Yard in Charlestown, Massachusetts, where we were greeted by Boatswain Mate 2nd Class (BM2) Philip Gagnon. Phil, as he requested we call him, escorted us on to the ship, where we were given the unique opportunity to watch the retreat ceremony carried out by the ship's crew. This ceremony signals the end of the duty day

Crew members aboard the USS *Constitution* preparing for the daily retreat ceremony—a.k.a. the striking of the colors or lowering of the flag—which signifies the end of the duty day and serves as a ceremony for "paying respect to the flag."

and pays respect to the American flag. The retreat ceremony is only conducted after the ship is closed to tourists for the day and is not normally witnessed by civilians.

Phil then escorted our team on a tour of the ship and also informed us that CDR Cooper had granted us full access to the entire ship during the two-night investigation. This was an extremely unique situation, as the standard tour of this historical ship only allows access to the top deck (spar deck) and sections of the main gun deck and the berthing deck. Our team was given full access to all of these locations, as well as the captain's quarters, tiller room, officers' quarters, orlop deck, surgeon's room, bread room, gun powder room, sail maker's room, and the cannon ball storage areas. Having full access to all of these areas was crucial to being able to conduct a proper investigation of the ship due to the experiences and the locations of those experiences reported by the ship's crew. This unusual access would also prove critical in our team's ability to validate the crew's own experiences, and in collecting some of our best evidence of paranormal activity to date.

During our tour one thing became very apparent: setting up the infrared DVR cameras was going to be difficult. The entire inside of the ship is painted gloss white, which causes a great deal of glare in enclosed locations, such as the captain's quarters and the tiller room. Another minor issue was that some of the lights on the ship had to be left on because one of the crew not involved with the investigation still had to come on board at midnight to check the bilge pump down on the orlop deck. We were able to turn off some of the lights on the main gun deck and in the tiller room, on the berthing deck, and in the officers' quarters. The lights had to be left on in the captain's quarters, sail maker's room, surgeon's room, and on the orlop deck.

To keep any potential noise contamination to a minimum we set up our base camp in a small room near the sail maker's room on the orlop deck of the ship. From there we ran the camera cables for the DVR up the hatchways to the tiller room, officers' quarters, and main gun deck.

We began our investigation at approximately 10:30 p.m. on June 25, 2010. Beck Gann and I went to the captain's quarters on the main gun deck to conduct an EVP session, while Ellen MacNeil and Sharon Koogler conducted an EVP session in the surgeon's room two decks below us and Sarah and Phil remained at base camp, monitoring the DVR system.

We entered the captain's quarters through the port door (the left side door as you face the bow of the ship). We initially thought we were getting some

The setup of our four DVR cameras for the investigation (top left to bottom right): CH1 is the berthing deck, looking toward the bow of the ship; CH2 is the tiller room on the berthing deck, behind the officers' quarters; CH3 is the officers' quarters; CH4 is the main gun deck looking aft toward the captain's quarters.

activity on this door, as it seemed to move on command, but after a while we were able to debunk this slight movement as a breeze coming through a port gun opening across from the open door. To be sure of this I closed the door securely and asked whomever might be there to open the door, but nothing happened.

It is very important to understand that this door was securely closed during our hour and a half investigation of this area to comprehend what occurred at the end of this EVP session. The starboard door was open about three to four inches and we left it that way. We had been investigating the captain's quarters approximately thirty minutes when Beck was the first team member to have a personal experience. We had been asking the typical opening questions, such as, "If anyone is hear please give us a sign. Knock on something or make a noise." I was filming the room with my handheld IR mini-DV when I turned and saw that Beck was looking at the starboard door, and she seemed surprised and puzzled. I asked her what was wrong, and she told me she thought she had just seen something. I told her there were reports from the crew of shadow figures being seen on this deck, but she interrupted me, saying no, she thought she saw the face of a boy peeking through the partially open door as she pointed toward the starboard door.

I made my way to the door, opened it, and asked if there was anyone there, and it was at that moment I thought I heard someone answer me. I told

Still Image 1 taken from the video when Beck reacted to seeing the face of a "boy" peeking through the door in the background.

Still Image 2 from the video. Notice the expression on Beck's face. She was also speechless at this moment, as I asked her what had happened. Seeing the face of that boy is something she has not and likely will never forget.

whomever it might be that I thought I heard them, and also told them I needed to know their name. At that moment, I did not hear a response or see anything except my own shadow to the right past the cannon, but what was caught on the mini-DV camera I was carrying was the voice of a young boy saying, "By the door." Just seconds before that a shadow figure is also seen moving past me in front of the camera. This would be the first of several relevant and intelligent EVPs captured on the main gun deck during our investigation, as well more shadow figure movement, and that door movement on command. The response "By the door" in relation to my question "I need to know your name" was extremely significant, as by that door where Beck saw the face of this boy is a listing of all of the crew members that died on the ship.

From the birth of the Continental Navy by an act of Continental Congress on October 13, 1775, through the mid-1800s, young boys between ages six and sixteen could serve as crew members. In 1875, the minimum enlistment age of apprentice boys was changed to fourteen, with the maximum age at eighteen, and they served until their twenty-first birthday; this apprentice program was ended in 1904.

In the early years of the US, families who were struggling to get by would often look to apprentice their young boys into military service. Being in the service was often a better option for many of these male children. In the Navy, these young boys were also given the official designation "Boy" and would be able to move up in rank once they completed their apprenticeship. Boys were often given the duty of carrying cannon balls, gun powder, and other items up from the ship's stores deep inside the hull, as the hatchways to those areas were small; the Boys were also small, and could move quickly up and down through the small openings. For the most part Boys were well treated for the conditions of those days, and contrary to some beliefs, they were not raped by older crew members, as the American Navy treated that as a crime punishable by death. Also the older crewmen would often treat the boys like their sons or younger brothers, as they were away from their own families for so long. This is not to say that life was not tough, dangerous, and sometimes harsh aboard ship, but it was also a very good life in comparison to the conditions these boys came from. As for the USS *Constitution*, the ship's records confirm that from 1804 through 1825, five Boys attached to the ship died while in her service. What follows are the actual historical records:

1. 1804 - Boy David Darling died in a fall.

2. 1811 - Boy Abraham Harding died and was buried ashore in Cherbourg, France.

3. 1821 - Boy Solomon Gardner died in hospital ashore at Gibraltar.

4. 1822 - Boy Richard Organ fell overboard and was lost.

5. 1825 - Boy Joseph Colson died; buried ashore at Messina, Sicily.

It is very important to understand that at the time of our first night investigating the ship, we did not have any of this information. The fact that boys had once served on the ship would not be revealed to us until after discussing Beck's experience later that night with our escort, BM2 Philip Gagnon.

While this activity was happening on the main gun deck, Ellen and Sharon were having their own experiences in the surgeon's room on the orlop deck. While conducting an EVP session in the surgeon's room, Sharon and Ellen could hear footsteps and mumbled voices above them in the officers' quarters on the berthing deck. They even radioed up to Beck and I to see if it was us they were hearing, but at that time we were two decks above them in the map room. We know that it could not have been us they heard, as the recorder we left in the officers' quarters did not pick up any voices or footsteps during that hour of the investigation, and neither did Ellen's or Sharon's recorders, although they did hear these things with their own ears, so that in itself is strange. Is it possible that what Ellen and Sharon heard was us? Yes, although unlikely, and the evidence that was captured on the second night in the officers' quarters would make it even more likely that what they heard was paranormal in nature, rather than from any natural source.

The last and most compelling personal experience to occur on the first night's investigation was experienced by BM2 Gagnon, Beck, and myself in the captain's quarters on the main gun deck. Beck and I were at the end of our EVP session on that deck and we were getting ready to head back down to base camp when Phil walked through the starboard door where Beck had

The orlop deck, where several EVPs were captured.

The surgeon's room behind the orlop deck. This room is directly below the officers' quarters.

seen the boy's face and that had been closing on command for us. The port door was still closed and latched. Phil asked us if we had any activity happening, and I told him about the door closing for us; he suggested it might be the tide causing it and asked us if we had asked for the door to open. I told him no and suggested that he use his commanding voice and give an order to anyone that might be there to open the door.

While we were referring to the starboard door that was still partially open about six inches—Phil had not closed it behind him—someone else seemed to think Phil was referring to the port door when he gave his order to, "Open that door!" We all heard the port door latch click as the door handle turned and then the door swung completely open on to the main gun deck. I was standing about six feet from the door at the port end of the large table in the captain's quarters when this happened. Beck was on the opposite side of the table from me, and Phil was standing near the starboard door, as he had been facing it when he gave his order.

At that moment I began to smile, until I realized I had already shut off my handheld video camera and digital recorder and did not capture any of it! I looked across at Beck and her expression was one of surprise, but she was holding her ground. When I looked over at Phil, I knew he was in shock and perhaps a bit frightened by what had just happened. He looked at me and asked me in a broken voice, "That . . . door . . . just . . . opened . . . didn't it?" I told him yes, and I found that I was still smiling when I answered him. Unlike Phil, I was excited by what had just occurred, and was also hoping that my reaction to it might calm his own, but that was not the case. I asked Phil if he was okay and he simply responded, "I have to go now," and literally left the room, walked up to the spar deck, and left the ship.

I immediately called down to Ellen on my walkie and told her what happened, and we left to go check on Phil. We found Phil just down on the dock, having a cigarette and taking with another crew member, Aviation Boatswain's Mate Aircraft Handler Airman (ABHN) Mark Alexander, who would be our escort during the second night.

Upon talking with him, it was obvious that Phil was shaken by this experience. We did our best to ease his concerns about what might be on board the ship by reminding him that even if it was a spirit that had opened the door, it only did so upon his command, if in fact it was a spirit at all that caused the door to open. Since we were still in the middle of conducting our investigation, we were not yet ready to make any determinations about anything happening

The main gun deck looking at the door to the captain's quarters. This is the door that was closed and latched, but opened on its own on command of Boatswain Mate 2nd Class (BM2) Philip Gagnon during the investigation.

being paranormal in nature or otherwise. Too much work still needed to be done, and data still needed to be collected and later reviewed. We also still had a second night of investigation ahead of us.

After a short break and some additional discussion and joking about his experience with Mark, Phil was ready to get back on the ship and see what else we might experience. Unfortunately, the rest of the first night seemed rather quiet, with no other obvious activity experienced by any of our investigators or Phil, but we still had hours of audio and video to review which might tell another story. We wrapped up the first night's investigation at about 2:00 a.m. on June 26, 2010.

June 26, 2010, 2:30 A.M. to 7:00 A.M., Summerville, Massachusetts

I arrived at my hotel in Summerville, Massachusetts, still pumped up from the investigation and the experiences we had in just the first night alone. Since I knew I was not going to be able to sleep anytime soon and we did not have to be back at the ship until 7:00 p.m., I decided to start going through at least some of the audio and video from the captain's quarters.

After settling in my room, I unpacked my laptop and the digital audio recorder I had used in the captain's quarters. I use WavePad Sound Editor® audio software installed on my laptop to review all of our audio, so I plugged the recorder in via USB cable and downloaded the audio files.

Whenever recording audio, I always use an uncompressed high quality format such as .wav if the recorder supports it; if not I look to use .wma over .mpg. Always use the highest quality settings possible to ensure you are getting the best audio out of your recorder. It makes a huge difference when trying to capture Electronic Voice Phenomenon (EVPs).

When reviewing audio, I also use a good pair of over-the-ear headphones rather than earbuds, as the sound quality is much better and they block out most of the ambient background noise in a room; I do not use sound canceling headphones, as they can cancel out some sounds from the audio you are listening to, meaning there is a possibility they can cancel out EVPs. Once I have found what I believe are EVPs, I then listen to them without headphones at a volume of about seventy to eighty percent. If I can clearly hear the EVP through the computer's speakers, then I will classify it as a Class A EVP. If I need to boost the volume to hear it, even if I am not sure what is being said, then I consider it a Class B. If I have to go back to the headphones and increase the volume then I consider it a Class C EVP. I typically throw out Class C EVPs, as I personally consider them unreliable to present as evidence.

So there I sat at the desk in my hotel room, headphones pasted to my ears, listening to the audio recorded in the map room. The first forty-five to fifty minutes revealed nothing unusual, but this is the way it goes with trying to capture paranormal activity. I always say that reviewing evidence is like watching grass grow: it is boring as hell, takes hours on end, and is the part of paranormal investigation that they really do not show you on ghost hunting reality shows.

The positive side of doing the data review is that you are the first one to hear any EVPs or see any unusual video or photo evidence that was captured. Those are glorious and exciting moments, and well worth the many hours spent reviewing all of the audio, photo, and video data.

For this particular investigation, I did not have to wait all that long before I heard the first EVP. I was a little over forty-five minutes into the audio when I heard a response to my question, "I need to know your name." What I heard was the voice of what sounded like a young teenage boy saying something, but I could not quite make it out. It then dawned on me that at this point in the audio I had also been filming with my handheld mini-DV camera, so I pulled out the camera, downloaded the video to my laptop, and pulled up the footage. I watched and listened as the camera footage moved toward the port door where Beck stated she had just seen the face of a young boy.

I watched as I opened the starboard door from the captain's quarters on to the main gun deck, and what I saw just a moment after opening the door surprised me. There, moving from left to right and then disappearing into the shadows, was a shadow figure! I continued to watch and listen for several more seconds when I came to the part where I asked the question, "I need to know your name." This time the response came loud and clear over the video's audio; it was the voice of a young boy saying, "By the door." At that moment chills shot up my spine, as I remembered that by that exact door was a listing of all the names of the crew members that had died while serving on board the ship.

At this point I decided to go to the website for the Constitution Museum and attempt to do some research on the ship's crew. As it happened, I did find many of the ship's logs online from her early years. This is where I found the records on the Boys who had died while in the ship's service. I wrote the names down so that during the second investigation I could try asking the spirit which name was his in hopes of actually identifying this individual. At this point I could feel exhaustion coming over me. It was just about 7:00 a.m. on January 26, and it was time to get some sleep before the second night's investigation.

26 June 2010, 7:00 p.m., Charlestown, Massachusetts

Our team met for dinner at 5:00 p.m. before heading to the ship. Since our equipment was already set up on the ship, we did not need to arrive as early as we did the first night. We arrived at the Navy Yard at approximately 7:00 p.m., and were greeted by Aviation Boatswain's Mate Aircraft Handler Airman (ABHN) Mark Alexander, who would be our escort for the night. Mark, as he requested we call him, was very excited about investigating with us. He told us he was hoping to have an experience at least similar to the one Phil had

The USS *Constitution* on the second night of the investigation (June 26, 2010) at her docking pier in the Charlestown Navy Yard, Charlestown, Massachusetts.

with the door opening on command. We were excited by his enthusiasm and invited him to participate in our EVP sessions. It was probably the smartest decision we made that entire weekend, but that would not be obvious until we reviewed all of our data.

We began our investigation at 8:30 p.m. in the captain's quarters. I asked for the boy whom Beck had seen the night before to join us and please let us know which of the names I was about to read off was his. I read from the list of five boys who had died in the ship's service, reading one name at a time and allowing several seconds in between for an answer. I immediately reviewed the audio at the end of the session, but there was no response to any of the names and no other EVPs had been captured. We tried again but with the same results.

From there we moved on to the main gun deck outside the captain's quarters. Mark was with us, and asked if we would like him to go through a standard gun drill. We all agreed that would be a great idea. Mark, in a clear commanding voice, yelled out the following orders for the gun drill:

One of the thirty 24-pounder main guns of the USS *Constitution*. On its carriage each of these guns weighs about 6,400 pounds and had an effective range of approximately 1,200 yards, firing a solid iron shot weighing twenty-four pounds. During her service from 1798–1802, the ship was also outfitted with an additional sixteen 18-pounder and fourteen 12-pounder guns.

1. Beat to Quarters!
2. Silence!
3. Cast loose your gun!
4. Run in your gun!
5. Sponge your gun!
6. Load the cartridge!
7. Wad your cartridge and ram home!
8. Shot your gun!
9. Wad your shot and ram home!
10. Run out your gun!
11. Two Six!
12. Two Six!
13. Two Six!
14. That's well!
15. Prick and prime!
16. Wipe dry!

17. Lay on your apron!
18. Point your gun!
19. That's well!
20. Remove your apron!
21. Stand by!
22. Fire!

The order "Stand by" was the most significant of all the orders, as that would be the only one a crewman would responsd to. That response would be, "Standing by" which, during our data review, was the exact EVP response we captured on our audio. It was again the same voice of the young boy that we had captured on the first night, but this would not be the last time we would hear his voice in an EVP interacting with Mark.

Shortly after this gun drill exercise we decided to break up the team into smaller groups. Sarah and I stayed on the main gun deck with Mark, while Sharon and Ellen headed down to the berthing deck to conduct a quick EVP session; we would all meet back at base camp in thirty minutes to regroup. Mark gave Sara and me a more detailed tour of the forward part of the main gun deck around the kitchen area. He described to us how in the 1800s, they would keep live animals on the ship for food, such as cows, pigs, and chickens. I had my audio recorder going, as well as another one set up on this section of the deck near the stove, and it was a good thing, because the EVP that we captured at that moment is what I feel to this day is the most important and interactive EVP we have ever captured. Again, we captured the voice of that same boy saying, "And a bear" right after Mark finished describing the type of animals that were kept on the ship. This is a Class A, very clear EVP, and it made the jaws of the commander and officers drop when they heard it at the reveal.

What makes this EVP even more compelling is that although this boy most likely died in the 1800s, the black bear mascot referred to as Commodore Scrappy did not sail on the ship until her world cruise from 1934 to 1936. So this begs the question, how is the spirit of a boy who died in the 1800s aware of a bear that sailed on the ship in the 1930s? The only probable explanation for this is that the spirit of this boy has retained his intelligence; he is still able to interact, learn, and understand everything that is going on around him, even to the point where he follows commands and helps to give tours of the ship.

The kitchen and manger area of the main gun deck, where live animals were kept for food on the ship during the 1800s. This is also the area where the Class A EVP of a boy's voice was captured.

This boy's willing participation in the daily routines of the ship and our investigation confirms that we do still continue to exist even after our bodies fail us. After our physical form is gone, what makes us who we are lives on and is able to continue and interact, at least in some way, with the physical world; this boy and his interactions with us are proof of life after death. Granted, this is a bold statement, but how else can we explain this? The only other explanations would be that I am a liar, that I faked the evidence, or that I have made all of this up. My defense to this is that I was not the only person on that ship for two nights and our team was supervised by a ship's officer both nights, one of whom witnessed his own paranormal experience along with us. Also, the US Navy is not prone to just accepting someone's word about something without believable proof of their statements.

This would not be the most compelling evidence of paranormal activity we would capture on the ship over the two nights. During the second night's investigation we decided to try an experiment of sorts. Since on the previous night while conducting an EVP session in the surgeon's room Ellen and Sharon heard voices and footsteps coming from the officers' quarters above them, we decided to repeat an EVP session in the surgeon's room while at the same time having one of us just sit in the officers' quarters and observe. Ellen and Sharon conducted the EVP session and we had Sarah sit in the officers' quarters. What we captured on our DVR camera in the officers' quarters during this experiment still fascinates us to this very day. Trying to explain it is difficult, so I have included several photos from the video to help.

Sarah's orders were to sit in the officers' quarters with a recorder and in view of the DVR camera. She was to do nothing except listen and watch while Ellen and Sharon conducted an EVP session in the surgeon's room below her. Sarah was to listen and watch for anything unusual, and she would be the only person on that deck and the decks above her, so there should be no one walking around or talking. Ellen and Sharon would be sitting in the room below her, and at most she would only hear them talking; she was to report if she did hear them. Mark and I would be at base camp, watching the monitors with two other female crew members who had asked if they could observe for an hour or so.

About twenty minutes into the session Sarah reported that she could not hear Ellen or Sharon below her and nothing else had occurred. Unfortunately, Mark and I were distracted from watching the DVR monitor by discussions with the other two crew members about the investigation and about paranormal investigating, and we did not see what was captured by the camera in the officers' quarters when the event occurred, although neither did Sarah, even though she was looking right at it.

As seen in the photos (opposite), Sarah was sitting at one of the tables in the center of the officers' quarters, and this is where she sat from the time she settled into the room. As identified in the first still photo (right) from the DVR footage, on the table in front of Sarah is a digital recorder, KII meter, and a flashlight. She also had a walkie-talkie to communicate with base camp. As Sarah had done on and off during her hour in the room, at 10:17 p.m. and 25 seconds per the DVR footage, she looks up in the direction of the mirrored dresser and the berthing deck. At 10:17 p.m. and 27 seconds a light anomaly begins to manifest in a location somewhere between the far end of the table from Sarah and the left side of the mirrored dresser. We have determined that it is manifesting somewhere in the space between these items, as a reflection of the anomaly can be seen in the top of the table as it grows brighter and moves higher, and before it disappears. From 10:17 p.m. and 27 seconds until 10:17 p.m. and 29 seconds, the light anomaly appears to not only spiral upward,

A still photo pulled from the DVR camera in the officers' quarters. Note the items Sarah had on the table with her in the room and none are in her possession.

The light anomaly (circled) suddenly appears just as Sarah looks up from the table, but she does not see this light—it is only visible in the infrared light spectrum of the DVR camera. To view this video, go to our website at http://www.spiritsofnewengland.org/evidence.html.

but also grow in size and intensity until it suddenly collapses into itself and disappears. At its greatest it appears to be about the size of a large grapefruit before it collapses into itself. Finally, at 10:17 and 33 seconds, Sarah looks back down at the walkie-talkie in her hand.

Although Sarah was looking in the exact direction of the anomaly, she had no reaction to it and never saw it. It was only visible and captured in the infrared spectrum of the DVR camera. The more we watch this footage the stranger and more compelling it becomes.

One of the last pieces of visual evidence we captured was in a photograph taken on the berthing deck about one hour after the DVR captured the strange light anomaly. The only investigator on that deck at the time was me (Jack Kenna); everyone else was a deck below at base camp. I was just coming back from the officers' quarters, where I picked up the KII meter and audio recorder that Sarah left there.

I noticed that the berthing deck just did not feel right. It was as if I was being watched. I remembered that this was one of the claims made by crew members, so I decided to take some pictures of the deck. Out of probably twenty or more photos taken on this deck, only one picked up something unusual. In the photo (opposite) you can see something odd in the circled area (and in the original color photo it has a bluish hue) by one of the support beams of the deck. When we zoomed in on this section, we can clearly see that this bluish object seems to have movement while everything around it is still. There is also nothing on that deck that would give off a bluish reflection.

To be sure this might possibly be something paranormal in nature, we sent the original digital image and the zoomed copy to a friend of ours who was also a paranormal investigator at the time and had many years of experience reviewing and analyzing photo evidence of potential paranormal activity. Her opinion was that the movement and color of the item did not make sense to the rest of the items in the photo. She felt that whatever it was looked like it was either moving behind the support or coming from behind it. She did agree that this could be something paranormal. Given the other events and experiences of the previous night and that night, we agreed with her statements. While photos are always interesting, they represent only a single moment in time. This photo is very compelling, and added one more piece to the puzzle of providing answers to the officers and crew of the USS *Constitution*.

The Findings

Due to scheduling and events on the USS *Constitution*, we were not able to present our findings to CDR Timothy M. Cooper and his officers until August 2010.

Photo taken on the berthing deck which captured this odd anomaly (circled). The full color photo can be viewed on our website at http://www.spiritsofnewengland.org/evidence.html.

When we presented our evidence to CDR Cooper and his officers at the reveal, the commander delayed going to another meeting to hear all of our presentation. While in the end we were able to validate many of the experiences reported by the ship's officers and crew, which delighted many of them to no end, CDR Cooper was a bit more reserved in his response to our findings, even stating that he was hoping that we either would not have found anything, or that it would have been one of the ship's notable captains from her historic past. In the end CDR Cooper accepted, again a bit reluctantly, our professional conclusion that the USS *Constitution* does have legitimate paranormal activity occurring onboard, and that the spirits of at least some of the ship's past crew members still reside aboard, watching over her and her current crew, and at times even attempting to interact with officers and crew for the benefit of the ship.

Public Access to the Ship

The USS Constitution is normally open to the public year-round, with the exception of Martin Luther King Jr.'s birthday, Thanksgiving Day, Christmas

One of the guns on the top spar deck the first night of the investigation. Crew members reported finding small, wet, bare footprints on this deck, but no one is allowed to go barefoot on the ship. They were found in the morning before the ship was open to visitors and started and stopped around the center of the deck.

Team member Sarah Campbell investigating the powder storage area in the belly of the *Constitution*. Notice this room is clad in copper to prevent any sparking or fire. Almost all of this is the original copper installed during the ship's construction.

Team member Sharon Koogler investigating the bread room (food storage area) in the bottom stern area of the ship. Several "colorful" EVPs were captured in this area.

Day, and New Year's Day. In March 2015, she was moved from her berth at Pier 1 West into Dry Dock #1 in Charlestown Navy Yard, Charlestown, Massachusetts, for repairs. On July 23, 2017, after the early completion of all her repairs, the USS *Constitution* was towed from Dry Dock #1 to Pier 1 East. On August 2, 2017, she returned to her home at Pier 1 West. You can check on status and hours of operation at https://ussconstitutionmuseum.org.

Investigator Insights

In discussing this book with the other members of the team, a lot of ideas were kicked around for a way to make it stand out a bit more from books in this same genre. One idea that particularly stood out was from the team's founder, Ms. Ellen MacNeil. She suggested I include comments and insight from each team member for each of the investigations.

Although doing this for every investigation would be cumbersome, I felt it would be a perfect thing to do for the USS *Constitution*, given the historical nature of this investigation and the magnitude of it. I know that it had a profound and meaningful impact on all of us who investigated the ship, as well as on the officers who were with us during the investigation. What follows is my interview with the S.P.I.R.I.T.S. team and their responses.

Question: So what was each of your first reactions when you found out the team was approved to investigate the USS *Constitution*?

Sharon Koogler: Excited!

Sarah Campbell: Somehow saying excited just does not quite cover that first reaction for me. There was a mesh of emotions that collided all at once. Being an avid sailor from a young age, the thought of investigating on a ship converted me into a squealing fangirl state a bit. Yet this was not just a ship, it was not just some boat on the harbor, this was the USS *Constitution*! This was the mother lode! The impossible became possible! It was so much more than just an investigation.

While any investigation, be it home or historical building, touches on a glimpse of the past, this one seemed like a step beyond that. This was history in action, and we were being allowed to be a part of something that helped create the world we live in today. Pride would be the final reaction given by this investigation, and it is something I believe will stay with us investigators for the rest of our days. Not only in what we did on the USS *Constitution*, but for the team being able to take on such a daunting task and handle it with such proficiency.

Ellen MacNeil: Seriously, I let out a loud "Whoop!" in shock and delight, and did my happy dance all over my office, much to the chagrin of my coworkers.

Beck Gann: When Ellen told me we were investigating the USS *Constitution* I was extremely excited! I could not believe it was happening! We were so lucky to have this honor of investigating the *Constitution*. I felt proud.

Jack Kenna: Dumbfounded. When Ellen first told me she had sent an e-mail request to the ship's office and they wrote back saying they were very interested in having the ship investigated, I just did not get too excited about it; I knew it would still have to go to the commander, and then he would have to get approval from his higher ups, so I did not expect it would really happen. But then, when she forwarded us the e-mail from their office telling us we were approved by the Navy to conduct the investigation, my jaw just dropped and I was speechless.

Question: What is your most vivid memory of this investigation?

Sharon: The jellyfish surrounding the ship at her dock! Seriously though, standing on the ship's deck while they lowered the colors—that was truly amazing and special to me.

Sarah: So many memories stand out about that investigation it is hard to just pick one, but I would say the memory of sitting alone in a room, in the dark, all by myself for an hour. This will always be one of the first things that sticks out in my mind. Not because of anything that happened; it was simply the situation itself. A lifetime filled with horror movies causes the mind to wander in a pitch black room.

A good portion of the time I spent in that room was in pure anticipation of something reaching out and touching my shoulder or flicking my hair. Anything—just the slightest touch—while it probably would have given me a heart attack, it would have made for good "personal experience" footage. Looking back on that night and following it up with the evidence captured in that room with me, I find it wild to know that there was actually someone, or more than one, in the room with me. Turns out I was not alone for an hour after all.

Ellen MacNeil: My most vivid memory would have to be of Beck seeing the face of a little boy peeking around the door into the captain's quarters. Although we did not capture the boy on video, Beck's reaction of disbelief speaks for itself.

Beck Gann: My most vivid memory was seeing a little boy peek around the door to the captain's quarters. Jack and I had been in the captain's quarters, asking for one of the doors to be moved, and one of the two doors into the room did move. We went over, checked the door, and thought maybe it was a breeze moving it, so we turned away from the door. I happened to look back—I am not sure why—and saw the face of a blonde-haired little boy peeking through the opening in the door. It blew my mind! It was very clear and vivid to me.

He looked to be about ten years old. It is still clear in my mind to this day. I am Christian, and I was taught that to be absent from the body means to be with God, so this experience did shake me up, but I am glad that Jack caught me on video—my expression says it all.

Jack: Standing six feet from the closed and latched door in the captain's quarters with Boatswain Mate 2nd Class (BM2) Philip Gagnon and Beck when Phil gave the order to "Open that door!" and I heard the latch turn and watched that closed door slowly and steadily open wide on to the main gun deck. I will never forget that or Phil's reaction afterward.

Question: What is your favorite piece of evidence from this investigation and why?

Sharon: The voice that mimicked me; I made a weird growl sound and someone mimicked it! That was pretty awesome.

Sarah: A biased answer would be any piece of evidence caught with a profanity in it screams out favorite. Partly just for the laughs of it, but there is a certain authenticity brought to the table when you catch sailors talking like the stereotypical sailor. It was just sailors being sailors. If it had not been for this investigation, I am not sure I would have ever questioned if sailors dropped the "f" bomb three hundred years ago.

Ellen: My favorite piece of evidence has to be the odd light we captured on our DVR camera in the officers' quarters. My daughter Sarah was in there at the time it happened, and on the video she is even looking right in the direction it appears, but she never saw it at the time, not until we reviewed the footage anyway. What is amazing is that there is no light source for this anomaly, and it only showed up in the infrared light spectrum.

Beck: My own personal experience of seeing the face of that little boy. It really had a major impact on me.

Jack: It is an EVP captured on the main gun deck during the second night's investigation. I discuss it in the chapter. It is the voice of a young boy saying, "And a bear." Once you know the history of the ship, it is obvious the boy is referring to the ship's mascot from the 1930s International Tour, a black bear cub named Commodore Scrappy by the crew.

What impresses me most about this EVP is that it is interacting with us, helping the officer with us that night to give us a tour. It is also fascinating that the spirit of a boy who very likely died in the 1800s knows about a bear that was kept on the ship in the 1930s. To me, this single EVP is proof that our souls, our intelligence—who we really are—lives on after our bodies have failed us.

Question: Is there any aspect of this investigation that you either regret, or wish you or the team had done differently?

Sharon: One of the team made a mistake when reviewing some of the video that resulted in the loss of some evidence. It was just a mistake, and had no real impact on the final results of the investigation, but what was lost could have validated the personal experience of the officer who was with us the first night. It is just one of those things that you wish had not happened. Other than that, no, I would not change a thing about how we managed the investigation.

Sarah: There are only two things, and neither one of them could have really been changed. One, I wish I had actually seen the "orb" or light go by the mirror in the officers' quarters while I was sitting in the dark room by myself. Despite the scare it would have given me, it would have been truly fascinating to see.

The only other thing would be that I wish the camera Jack was holding had actually been facing Beck when she saw the face of the little boy by the door. While the video we currently have is utterly priceless, actually capturing the boy on camera when he showed himself would have been absolutely fantastic.

Ellen: I wish we had the equipment that we have now and more time, but real regrets, none.

Beck: I am proud of the way our team handled the entire case and there is nothing I would change, although I do wish that Jack had seen the little boy, too.

Jack: No, there is nothing I regret or would change. We all acted as professionals, we captured some fantastic and compelling evidence of the haunting on the ship, and we conducted our investigation and our reveal to the commander and his officers in a respectful and professional manner.

Question: What are you most proud of about this investigation personally and regarding the team?

Sharon: That we were allowed to do it at all! I think the team did a great job not only investigating, but debunking as well, and that we respected the wishes of CDR Cooper and did not post the findings on our website or Facebook® for five years.

Sarah: Above all else, our ability to handle the case turned into the greatest achievement we could have in my eyes. The reveal, which is where the pride really came in. Seeing the reaction to the evidence captured by not only the captain but also the crew just spoke of the story of why we do what we do.

Ellen: I feel that we gave our hearts to this investigation, and we were humbled by the opportunity to show CDR Cooper and the Navy how dedicated, passionate, and professional we are when we conduct our investigations.

Beck: I am very proud of our whole team for the way we handled ourselves and the investigation. We proved to a lot of people and our peers that we are professionals, and we can handle any investigation given to us just as well as the bigger, more well-known paranormal teams that are out there.

Jack: Again, I am very proud of the fact that we all acted professionally before, during, and after the investigation and the reveal. For five years we respected the verbal wishes of then CDR Timothy M. Cooper, the first commander of the ship in her new congressional role as "America's Ship of State," to not post information about our investigation on our website or other online media.

Now, given the fact that there have been two new commanders of the ship since CDR Cooper's change of command in July 2011, and given the fact that the ship will be going into dry dock and will be closed to the public for repairs until 2018, we feel it is time to share this investigation and our findings with the public, as we are sure that activity onboard the ship will increase during her repair period, as will rumors from uninformed crew and workers on the ship about it being haunted.

We feel it is important that people understand just who is haunting this great ship: previous crew members who still take pride in their ship, their home, and who look over her, her crew, and the visitors to what is the world's oldest commissioned Navy ship, "America's Ship of State," the USS *Constitution*.

Question: What impact did this investigation have on you, your life, or your beliefs?

Sharon: It was a great opportunity, perhaps once in a lifetime.

Sarah: Confirmation was the biggest impact of this investigation. To this day, I remain a skeptic on many things in the realm of the paranormal, but during those two nights and the evidence we caught, it told a story of the connections we grasp on to from life into the afterlife. Every time we go out on a "hunt" I am left fascinated and filled with questions about what lies ahead for us after death, but also questions like, "What kind of person does it take to become an intelligent haunting?" and "How does that person now see the world and the living?" I am always left wanting to know more.

Ellen: I was so touched by some of the audio evidence we captured, especially the young boy's voice saying "and a bear," adding to the list of animals that were kept on the ship that our escort on the second night was describing to Jack and Sarah. The bear was obviously very important to the boy, and the *Constitution* may have been the only home this boy and some of her other crew ever really knew.

Beck: I have had things happen in my life to make me question what comes after. I always believed you went to heaven when you died.

Now I have to say for whatever reason there are spirits that hang around. Maybe they have unfinished business.

Jack: For me it was a major milestone. Just a year earlier, I never would have imagined that our small team would have ended up conducting a paranormal investigation for the Navy on what was and is "America's Ship of State," what some Navy officers and Congress now refer to as the "US Navy's Flag Ship" because of her title. Even more of an impact on me and my beliefs in an afterlife and God were the EVPs we captured. After listening to all of them, I no longer have any doubt that who we are—our soul if you will—lives on after our physical bodies have failed us. I also no longer have any doubts in the existence of God, and it does not matter which God you believe in or if you just believe in a higher cosmic being, there is a part of us, perhaps a part of every living thing on this planet, that did not just evolve. Something or someone beyond our current human understanding introduced the spark of life into us, gave us our soul, and for me, I find comfort in referring to this higher being as God.

Question: What is your personal opinion and/or conclusion about the findings of the investigation? Do you think the ship is haunted? If yes, who do you think haunts it?

Sharon: It is absolutely haunted! From everything we caught I would say it is past crew members making sure all is well.

Sarah: I am not entirely sure that I could be convinced that the ship is not haunted at this point. Too many things happened while aboard the ship to allow my mind to say that there was nothing else on that ship. Without a doubt I believe the sailors of past crews still reside there.

Ellen: Is the USS *Constitution* haunted? Absolutely! I feel the ship is protected by former crew who responded to us playfully, respectfully, and with the same curiosity we had for them.

Beck: I believe the ship is haunted. Too many things happened, and I will never forget that blonde little boy looking at me. It made me sad and I felt bad for him. One thing is for sure, the captain's face when shown all of the evidence said it all. He had heard stories from his crew, but when he heard the EVPs and saw the video the look on his face was priceless. I felt so proud; what a great feeling. Our team did an awesome job.

Jack: Is the ship haunted? The findings are what they are, they speak for themselves. We captured spirit voices of what I believe are past crew members responding to and interacting with us. We captured on video things we cannot explain and did not even see at the time. All of this is solid evidence of a haunting, but that does not mean the spirits that are there are in any way harmful—just the opposite in this case.

Question: What impact do you feel the investigation had on the ship's officers and crew?

Sharon: It was definitely mixed. Everyone felt validated in the fact that we had the same experiences they had, like seeing the young boy and hearing voices and footsteps; on the other hand, the commander was hoping to hell we would find nothing.

Sarah: Like any investigation, I believe that our reveal helped prove that the client(s) were not actually going insane. Though we laugh over the idea, I believe that the reassurance that something does actually go bump in the night does make a huge impact. While in some cases I do believe we helped, I still feel bad for the person who has to deal with the bilge pump every night who has a mild fear of the ghosts that reside in that ship. It is not always easy to be brave in the dark. I just hope that person knows that the ghosts would be appreciative of his or her hard work, because that person is assisting in keeping those proud spirits alive and with us.

Ellen: We were able to validate so many of the claims of activity by the crew, much to the shock of the captain, whom I think did not expect us to find anything. As we ended our presentation to the officers I turned to the crew, who were high-fiving each other and giving us thumbs up, because we now had audio and video proof that they really were experiencing paranormal events on the ship.

Beck: What Ellen said! (Laughing)

Jack: I believe for many of the crew it was a validation of their own personal experiences on the ship. For some, it was a relief to finally know they were not imagining things, and that their commander finally had solid evidence presented to him to prove his crew was telling him the truth about experiences they had reported to him.

As for CDR Cooper, like Ellen said, he was actually hoping we would not find anything—he even said that—or if we had, he hoped that it was haunted by one of the ship's former captains, but in the end he was intrigued by our findings and even delayed another meeting to hear our entire one-and-a-half hour presentation; that in itself spoke volumes to me.

Being a civilian employee in the Army, I know for a fact that when a ranking officer delays his next meeting to finish hearing what you have to say you have their interest and their undivided attention. What you are saying is important to them. I know as a team we greatly appreciate the fact that CDR Cooper and the Navy gave us this great opportunity, and that he gave his undivided attention to our presentation and was impressed with our work and our findings.

Final Thoughts

While I have discussed many things in this book about investigating the paranormal and shared with you just a few of our S.P.I.R.I.T.S. team's investigations, there is vastly much more than that to the paranormal realm. My purpose here was twofold: to provide some basic information and guidance that can be helpful to those of you who investigate or want to investigate, and to leave a small part of me behind for my children, grandchildren, and perhaps even future generations of my family to remember, discuss, and ponder, "Who was this crazy man that tried to speak with invisible people in the dark?"

Perhaps this will inspire one of them to pursue their own passion. Perhaps it will inspire one of you. To any skeptics, the universe is a vast and unknown place, so keep an open mind and let some of it in. To the believers, I say faith is strength. Faith—believing in something—is the most important thing to have when investigating the paranormal and in life itself. The thing is, it does not matter what your faith is—Catholic, Christian, Judaism, Islam, Hinduism, Buddhism, Creationism, Wicca, etc. As long as you believe in something more than this physical world we live in, you will find a strength to draw upon that can guide you, protect you, and give you the courage to persevere.

Bibliography

"100th Anniversary, North Adams Mayor A. C. Houghton Dies Following Fatal Accident," http://www.berkshireeagleblogs.com/beyondthe-grave/2014/08/01/100th-anniversary-north-ad-ams-mayor-a-c-houghton-dies-following-fatal-accident. Retrieved 14 April 2014.

Allen, Orrin Peer. *Descendants of Nicholas Cady of Watertown, Mass., 1645–1910.* Published by the author, Palmer, Massachusetts. Press of C. B. Fiske & Co. 1910. https://archive.org/details/descendantsnich00allegoog. Retrieved 13 April 2016.

The Apostle John 20:24–29, 21st Century King James Version (KJ21), Copyright © 1994 by Deuel Enterprises, Inc.

Cady, Jane A. (Bradford) (1815), https://www.wikitree.com/wiki/Bradford-2009. Retrieved 20 April 2014.

Cady, Caroline Virginia, birth and death information, http://www.ancestry.com/genealogy/records/carolinevirginiacady_52845660. Retrieved 19 April 2014.

Crane, Ellery Bicknell. *Historic Homes and Institutions and Genealogical and Personal Memoirs of Worcester County Massachusetts.* Worcester Historical Museum, The Lewis Publishing Company 1907, Fairbanks. pp. 191–192, 487-490.

DigitalDowsing.com: EM Pump; https://www.digitaldowsing.com/product/em-pump. Retrieved 04 March 2013.

Dornberger, Walter. *V-2.* Ballantine Books, 1954, p. 14.

Doyle, Sir Arthur Conan. *Sherlock Holmes, A Study in Scarlet*, Part 1, chap. 3, p. 27.

Doyle, Sir Arthur Conan. *Sherlock Holmes, The Sign of Four*, Chap. 6, p. 111.

"Fairbanks House Historical Site," http://www.fairbankshouse.org. Retrieved 02 January 2012.

Hirsch, Robert. *Seizing the Light: A History of Photography.*

History of the USS *Constitution*, https://www.history.navy.mil/browse-by-topic/ships/uss-constitution-americas-ship-of-state/background-for-media/brief-history.html. Retrieved 24 June 2010.

Houghton, Laura Cordelia, 1867–1871, http://www.familyrecord.net/getperson.php?personID=I64292&tree=CorlissOrdway&tngprint=1. Retrieved 14 April 2016.

Houghton, Mary C. , 1877–1914, http://www.familyrecord.net/getperson.php?personID=I64295&tree=CorlissOrdway. Retrieved 14 April 2016.

Kings Handbook of Boston Harbor, third edition, 1888.

www.madehow.com/Volume-7/Laser-Pointer.html. Retrieved 19 February 2013.

MakeUseOf.com. "How Does a Digital Camera Work." Retrieved 14 February 2013.

Naughton, Russell (10 August 2004). "Kalman Tihanyi (1897–1947)." Monash University. Retrieved 23 March 2013.

Needham, Joseph. *Science and Civilization in China: Volume 4, Physics and Physical Technology, Part 1, Physics.* Taipei: Caves Books Ltd., 1986, p. 82.

Ogden, Tom. (1999). *The Complete Idiot's Guide to Ghosts and Hauntings.* Alpha Books, pp. 107–108.

Parapedia Paranormal Encyclopedia: Ovilus; http://parapedia.wikia.com/wiki/Ovilus. Retrieved 05 March 2013.

Parker, R. D. "Thermic balance or radiometer." US Patent No 1,099,199. June 9, 1914. Retrieved 22 March 2013.

Pierce, Capt. William (William Pearce), https://www.geni.com/people/CaptWilliam Pierce/6000000003650747953, William Pearce (c. 1595–1622) Genealogy. Retrieved 12 April 2013.

Potter's American Monthly: Illustrated Magazine of History, Literature, Science and Art, Vol. VII, No. 58, October 1876, Philadelphia, John E. Potter & Company, *The Historic Buildings of America* by Benson J. Lossing, LL. D., *The Fairbanks House*, Dedham, pp. 241–247.

Potter's American Monthly: Illustrated Magazine of History, Literature, Science and Art, Vol. VI, No. 54, June 1876, Philadelphia, John E. Potter & Company, *History and Reminiscences of the Philadelphia Navy Yard* by Henry M. Vallette, USS *Constitution*, pp. 407-412.

Rivers, Roger, and Lorraine Maloney. "Blackinton Through Times of Change." 06 June 2003, http://www.iberkshires.com/printerFriendly.php?story_id=10595. Retrieved 15 April 2014.

Spear, W. F. *History of North Adams, Mass. 1749–1885.* Hoosac Valley News Printing House 1885, https://archive.org/details/historyofnorthad-00spearich. Retrieved 20 April 2014.

Spud*Pickles; Ghost Radar®: Legacy; http://spudpickles.com/app/ghost-radar-legacy. Retrieved 16 March 2013.

Texas Instruments, 1966. "First FLIR units produced." http://www.ti.com. Retrieved 23 March 2013.

USS *Constitution* Ship Logs, 06 Dec 1798–08 June 1934, http://www.captainsclerk.info/shiplogs/shiplogs.html. Retrieved 24 June 2010.

USS *Constitution* National Cruise Scrapbook compiled by Franciezek "Frank" Prusz, 1931–1934, https://ussconstitutionmuseum.org/collections-history/library-and-manuscript/scrapbooks/ncs-1931-1934. Retrieved 24 June 2010.

S.P.I.R.I.T.S. of New England
CLIENT INVESTIGATION FORM

DATE:	

NAME:	
ADDRESS:	
CITY:	STATE:	ZIP CODE:
PHONE NO.:	CELL NO.:
EMAIL:	

OWNERS/OCCUPANTS NAMES (INCLUDING YOURSELF)	GENDER (M / F)	RELATIONSHIP	DATE OF BIRTH / AGE

STRUCTURAL INFORMATION

BUILDING TYPE: (CHECK ONE)	Detached Residence ☐	Duplex ☐	Condo ☐	Apartment ☐	Other ☐

DO YOU OWN OR RENT?							
NO. OF BEDROOMS:		BATHROOMS:		SQUARE FEET:		LOT SIZE (SQ. FT.):	

ADDITIONAL ROOMS & OTHER INFORMATION:

HOW MANY YEARS AND/OR MONTHS HAVE YOU LIVED AT THE LOCATION?

S.P.I.R.I.T.S. of New England
CLIENT INVESTIGATION FORM

ANY KNOWN HISTORY OF LOCATION? (STRUCTURAL CHANGES, PREVIOUS OCCUPANTS, OTHER PARANORMAL ACTIVITY, ETC.)

HAVE ANY OTHER BUILDINGS BEEN CONSTRUCTED ON THE SITE PREVIOUS TO THE CURRENT ONE? IF YES, EXPLAIN:

IS THERE ANY KNOWN HISTORY OF THE SURROUNDING AREA? (OLD SCHOOLS, GRAVE SITES, OLD COURTS, OLD CHURCHES, ETC.)

ARE THERE ANY ACCOUNTS OF PARANORMAL ACTIVITY AT YOUR PREVIOUS RESIDENCE?

WERE ANY TRAGEDIES OR DEATHS ASSOCIATED WITH THE IMMEDIATE AREA OR NEIGHBORHOOD? IF YES, EXPLAIN:

S.P.I.R.I.T.S. of New England
CLIENT INVESTIGATION FORM

IS THERE ANY DOCUMENTATION OF PREVIOUS PARANORMAL ACTIVITY? (NEWSPAPER CLIPPINGS, ETC.)

RELIGIOUS & MEDICAL BACKGROUND

WHAT, IF ANY, IS YOUR RELIGIOUS BACKGROUND? (BOTH FAMILY AND YOUR PRESENT RELIGIOUS STATUS)

ANY HISTORY OF ALCOHOL OR DRUG ABUSE?

ANY HISTORY OF MENTAL ILLNESS? IF YES, EXPLAIN:

ANY HISTORY OF SERIOUS TRAUMA? (NEAR DEATH, RAPE, ETC.)

S.P.I.R.I.T.S. of New England
CLIENT INVESTIGATION FORM

LIST ALL MEDICATIONS AND PRESCRIPTION ITEMS USED IN THE PAST THREE YEARS. INCLUDE ALL PRESCRIPTION DRUGS, OVER-THE-COUNTER DRUGS, PRESCRIPTION EYEGLASSES, CONTACT LENSES, ETC. PLEASE MAKE A SEPARATE LIST FOR EACH OCCUPANT.

HAVE ANYONE'S PRESCRIPTIONS CHANGED RECENTLY?

ANY OTHER FAMILY HISTORY YOU THINK IS IMPORTANT?

WHEN DID THE CURRENT DISTURBANCES BEGIN AND WHAT HAPPENED FIRST?

WHAT DID YOU THINK OF THESE DISTURBANCES?

S.P.I.R.I.T.S. of New England
CLIENT INVESTIGATION FORM

HAVE YOU LOOKED FOR ORDINARY, NORMAL EXPLANATIONS? WHAT MAKES YOU THINK IT'S PARANORMAL?

WHEN DID THE MOST RECENT INCIDENT OCCUR AND WHAT HAPPENED?

HAVE THE DISTURBANCES BEEN INCREASING IN FREQUENCY AND/OR SEVERITY SINCE THEY FIRST BEGAN?

ARE EVENTS MORE FREQUENT AT CERTAIN TIMES DURING THE 24 HOURS OF THE DAY THAN AT OTHERS? IF YES, WHAT TIMES?

IS THERE A PATTERN OF ANY KIND TO THESE DISTURBANCES THAT YOU'VE NOTICED (E.G., WHEN THE EVENTS OCCURRED, WHAT SORTS OF OBJECTS WERE AFFECTED, WHAT LOCATIONS WERE INVOLVED, WHO WAS AROUND AT THE TIME, ETC.)?

IS ACTIVITY MORE FREQUENT IN CERTAIN PLACES (FOR EXAMPLE, IN CERTAIN ROOMS OF THE HOUSE) THAN IN OTHERS? IF YES, WHERE?

S.P.I.R.I.T.S. of New England
CLIENT INVESTIGATION FORM

DO THE OCCURRENCES HAPPEN MORE FREQUENTLY IN THE PRESENCE OR VICINITY OF CERTAIN PERSONS THAN THEY DO WITH OTHERS? IF YES, STATE WHICH PEOPLE. ALSO, DO THE EVENTS TAKE PLACE WHEN THEY ARE NOT IN THE AREA?

HAVE THERE BEEN ANY WITNESSES FROM OUTSIDE THE HOUSEHOLD? WHAT DID THEY EXPERIENCE, AS FAR AS YOU KNOW?

HAS ANYONE EVER SEEN AN OBJECT START TO MOVE WHEN NO ONE WAS NEAR IT? IF YES, DESCRIBE ALL SUCH OCCURRENCES.

IF THERE HAVE BEEN UNEXPLAINED MOVEMENTS OF OBJECTS, WAS THERE ANYTHING STRANGE ABOUT THE MANNER IN WHICH THE OBJECTS MOVED OR STOPPED? (E.G., OBJECTS THAT MOVE AROUND CORNERS, OR HIT WITH UNUSUALLY GREAT FORCE, ETC.)

HAVE YOU OR ANYONE IN THE RESIDENCE EVER USED OR EXPERIMENTED WITH OUIJA BOARDS, SÉANCES, ETC.?

S.P.I.R.I.T.S. of New England
CLIENT INVESTIGATION FORM

HAVE YOU OR ANYONE IN THE RESIDENCE EVER USED OR EXPERIMENTED WITH BLACK MAGIC OR USED ANY TYPE OF WITCHCRAFT FOR PERSONAL GAIN? (E.G., MONEY, LOVE, FAME, ETC.) IF YES, PLEASE EXPLAIN:

HOW WOULD YOU LIKE TO BE HELPED?

S.P.I.R.I.T.S. of New England
CLIENT INVESTIGATION FORM

HAVE ANY OF THE OCCUPANTS ENCOUNTERED ANY OF THE FOLLOWING? (EXPLAIN ALL THAT APPLY)

1. Voices: ☐

2. Smells/Odors: ☐

3. Shadows: ☐

4. Orbs: ☐

5. Smoky Forms: ☐

6. Strong Random Thoughts: ☐

7. Strong Feelings/Emotions: ☐

8. Cold Spots: ☐

9. Hot Spots: ☐

10. Recent Death of Loved One: ☐

11. Recent Anniversary of Loved One's Death, Birthday, Anniversary, etc.: ☐

S.P.I.R.I.T.S. of New England
CLIENT INVESTIGATION FORM

12. Sounds (Walking, Running, Knocking, etc.): ☐

13. Door(s) Opening/Closing: ☐

14. Mood Changes, Especially in One Room: ☐

15. Conversations With Spirits: ☐

16. Conversations Between Spirits: ☐

17. Disappearing Objects: ☐

18. Objects Moving: ☐

19. Puberty of Family Member or Emotional Stress of Adolescents in Area: ☐

20. Renovations to Location: ☐

21. Electrical Disturbances (Frequent Light Bulb Burnouts, etc.): ☐

22. Problems with Appliances (TV, Radio, Stereo, Computers, Clocks, Microwave, etc.): ☐

23. Headaches or Dizziness: ☐

Author Jack Kenna, 2016

About the Author

Jack Kenna was born in Troy, New York, on 03 January 1963. He grew up in an area rich in history, legends, folklore, haunted graveyards, and Revolutionary War battlefields. Jack's interest in the paranormal started at a very young age, driven by the fact that his mother had many experiences of her own, which she often discussed with him.

The home he grew up in and now raises his own family in also helped to pique his interest in the paranormal. In addition to his wife and their seven children, it is also home to what he refers to as a friendly spirit who seems to watch over the family.

Early in the twenty-first century his interest in the paranormal was rekindled by the reality television series *Ghost Hunters*® and the scientific investigation methods utilized by *The Atlantic Paranormal Society*® (TAPS®). These methods are very similar to the type of engineering and scientific methods that Jack has been using on a daily basis for the past thirty-plus years in his career as a senior engineering technician for the Department of the Army. Beyond his technical expertise for the Army, Jack has extensive video and audio skills, and expertise